CHARLOTTE BRONTË

WW

CHARLOTTE BRONTË

Patsy Stoneman

NORTHCOTE
BRITISH COUNCIL

© 2013 by Patsy Stoneman

First published in 2013 by Northcote House Publishers Ltd, Horndon, Tavistock, Devon, PL19 9NQ, United Kingdom.
Tel: +44 (0) 1822 810066 Fax: +44 (0) 1822 810034.

British Library Cataloguing-in-Publication Data
A catalogue record for this book is available from the British Library

ISBN 978-0-7463-1195-0 hardcover
ISBN 978-0-7463-0856-1 paperback

Typeset by PDQ Typesetting, Newcastle-under-Lyme
Printed and bound in the United Kingdom

For Colin

'his mind is indeed my library'

Contents

Biographical Outline   ix

Abbreviations   xiii

1   Early Life and Early Writing   1

2   *The Professor*   18

3   *Jane Eyre*   30

4   *Shirley*   48

5   *Villette*   63

6   Readers and Reproducers   79

Notes   98

Select Bibliography   108

Index   111

Biographical Outline

1777	Patrick Brontë (then Brunty) born in Drumballyroney, County Down.
1802	He enters St John's College, Cambridge, with the patronage of Thomas Tighe.
1807	He is ordained priest and subsequently takes up a number of different curacies.
1811	He publishes *Cottage Poems*.
1812	*April*: as a minister in the west of Yorkshire, he experiences the Luddite attack on Rawfold's Mill which Charlotte recreates in *Shirley*.
	December: he marries Maria Branwell, a Methodist from Penzance.
1813	He publishes *The Rural Minstrel*.
1814	*January*: Maria Brontë is born at Hightown, Liversedge.
1815	*February*: Elizabeth Brontë is born at Hightown, Liversedge.
1816	*April*: CHARLOTTE BRONTË IS BORN at Thornton.
1817	*June*: Patrick Branwell Brontë (known as Branwell) is born at Thornton.
1818	Patrick Brontë's *The Maid of Killarney* is published.
	July: Emily Jane Brontë is born at Thornton.
1820	*January*: Anne Brontë is born at Thornton.
	April: the family move to Haworth, where Patrick is 'perpetual curate'.
1821	*September*: Maria Brontë (the mother) dies, probably from cancer. Elizabeth Branwell, her sister, comes from Penzance to nurse her and stays to take care of the children (who call her 'Aunt Branwell').
1824	*July*: The young Maria and Elizabeth go to the Clergy Daughters' School at Cowan Bridge, near Kirkby

	Lonsdale, Lancashire (the origin for Lowood School in *Jane Eyre*). Charlotte follows in August and Emily in November.
1825	Maria and Elizabeth return to Haworth to die from tuberculosis. Charlotte and Emily also return home.
1826	Patrick Brontë buys the toy soldiers who are the basis of the children's prolific early writing, founding the fictional 'Great Glass Town' in west Africa.
1831	Charlotte goes to Miss Wooler's school at Roe Head, Mirfield, and meets Ellen Nussey and Mary Taylor.
1832	Charlotte leaves Roe Head to teach Emily and Anne at home.
1834	The imaginary Duke of Zamorna leaves Glass Town to become King of Angria. Emily and Anne form their own imaginary country called Gondal.
1835	Charlotte returns to Roe Head School as a teacher. Emily, who goes as a pupil, returns home after three months, suffering from home-sickness, and is replaced by Anne, who leaves in December 1837.
1838	Charlotte leaves Miss Wooler's school, which has now moved to Dewsbury.
1839	Charlotte rejects a proposal of marriage from Henry Nussey and becomes a governess at Mrs Sidgwick's, Stonegappe, near Skipton, but leaves after three months. Rejects a proposal from David Pryce. Writes her 'Farewell to Angria'.
1841	Charlotte goes as governess to Mrs White of Upperwood House, Rawdon, but leaves after four months.
1842	Charlotte and Emily go to Brussels to perfect their French and German at the Pensionnat Heger. Charlotte falls in love with her married tutor, M. Heger. *September*: William Weightman, Patrick Brontë's very popular young curate, dies from cholera in Haworth. *October*: Martha Taylor, younger sister of Charlotte's friend Mary, dies from cholera in Brussels. Aunt Branwell dies in Haworth from an intestinal complaint. Charlotte and Emily return home, too late for their aunt's funeral.
1843	Charlotte returns to Brussels alone but is increasingly lonely.

1844	Charlotte returns to Haworth. M. Heger does not reply to her desperate letters.
1845	Anne leaves her position with the Robinson family at Thorp Green, where she has been governess since 1840. A month later Branwell is dismissed from his post in the same family, probably because of an affair with Mrs Robinson which leaves him histrionically inconsolable.
1846	Charlotte, Emily and Anne publish a volume of poems under the pseudonyms 'Currer, Ellis and Acton Bell'. They are well reviewed but do not sell.
1847	Charlotte's novel, *The Professor*, is repeatedly rejected but *Jane Eyre* is accepted by Smith, Elder & Co. and published in October, becoming an instant success. Emily's *Wuthering Heights* and Anne's *Agnes Grey*, already accepted by Thomas Newby, are published in December.
1848	*June*: Anne's second novel, *The Tenant of Wildfell Hall*, is published. Charlotte and Anne visit London to prove their separate identity. *September*: Branwell dies from bronchitis after self-neglect and abuse of alcohol and laudanum. *December*: Emily dies from tuberculosis, refusing medical treatment.
1849	*May*: Anne, also suffering from tuberculosis, makes a last trip to Scarborough with Charlotte and Ellen Nussey, where she dies four days later. *October*: Charlotte's novel, *Shirley*, is published.
1850	Charlotte's identity is now known and she begins to take part in literary life, meeting Elizabeth Gaskell and many others. She writes a 'Preface' and 'Biographical Notice' for a new edition of *Wuthering Heights* and *Agnes Grey*.
1853	*January*: Charlotte's novel, *Villette* is published after protracted depression and illness. She begins *Emma*.
1854	Charlotte marries Arthur Bell Nicholls, her father's curate, after she recognizes his profound emotion. She is favourably impressed by his Irish connections.
1855	*March*: CHARLOTTE DIES from excessive vomiting during early pregnancy.
1857	Elizabeth Gaskell publishes her *Life of Charlotte Brontë*,

xi

and Charlotte's first novel *The Professor*, is posthumously published.

1861   Patrick Brontë dies, aged 85, and Arthur Nicholls returns to Ireland.

Abbreviations

A.   Christine Alexander (ed.), *The Brontës: Tales of Glass Town, Angria, and Gondal: Selected Writings* (Oxford: Oxford World's Classics, 2010).

B.   Juliet Barker, *The Brontës* [1994] (2nd edition, London: Abacus, 2010).

JE   Charlotte Brontë, *Jane Eyre* [1847] ed. Margaret Smith, intro. Sally Shuttleworth (Oxford: Oxford World's Classics, 2008).

L.   Margaret Smith (ed.), *The Letters of Charlotte Brontë*. 3 vols, (Oxford: Clarendon Press, 1995-2004).

G.   Elizabeth Gaskell, *The Life of Charlotte Brontë* [1857] ed. Angus Easson (Oxford: Oxford World's Classics, 2009).

P.   Charlotte Brontë, *The Professor* [1857] ed. Margaret Smith and Herbert Rosengarten (Oxford: Oxford World's Classics, 2008).

S.   Charlotte Brontë, *Shirley* [1849] ed. Herbert Rosengarten and Margaret Smith, intro. Janet Gezari (Oxford: Oxford World's Classics, 2008).

V.   Charlotte Brontë, *Villette* [1853] ed. Margaret Smith and Herbert Rosengarten, intro. Tim Dolin (Oxford: Oxford World's Classics, 2008).

1

Early Life and Early Writing

'Take courage, Charlotte; take courage.' (G. 309)

These were the dying words of Charlotte Brontë's sister, Anne. As she died, in 1849, she knew that she was leaving Charlotte, aged 33, the sole survivor of six siblings. Their sister Emily had also wished for courage:

> 'Tis all that I implore
> In life and death, a chainless soul,
> With courage to endure.[1]

Charlotte and her sisters and brother had needed to summon courage to endure grief and bereavement from their earliest years. Their mother had died in 1821, when Charlotte was 5, brother Branwell 4, Emily 3 and Anne 1 year old. Their two elder sisters, Maria and Elizabeth, were only 7 and 6, but became to some extent mother-substitutes. Three years later, however, they were sent, with Charlotte and Emily, to the disastrously negligent Clergy Daughters' School (the Lowood of Charlotte's *Jane Eyre*) from which Maria and Elizabeth returned only to die in their turn, aged 11 and 10. Charlotte, now the eldest at 9 years old, and Emily, aged 7, rejoined Branwell and Anne at their home in Haworth, in the West Riding of Yorkshire.

Haworth was a place which outsiders then regarded as harsh, remote and even uncivilized. Often referred to as an isolated village, it was in fact a small industrial town producing woollen cloth. There were hand-loom weavers who worked in their cottages up and down the steep main street, and there were nearly twenty small textile mills down in the valley. The Brontës' father, however, was not a tradesman but Haworth's 'perpetual curate' (not quite a vicar, but more than a subordinate curate) and the Parsonage where they lived is somewhat apart from the

1

town, at the very summit of its cobbled street, facing the church and enclosed on two sides by the graveyard. Behind the house the seemingly limitless moors stretch away to the horizon.

From 1825, when Charlotte and Anne returned home, until 1831, when Charlotte again went away to school, the four remaining children lived in the Parsonage with their father, the Reverend Patrick Brontë, and their mother's sister, 'Aunt Branwell', who had left her home in distant Penzance to care for them. Viewed from outside, it seemed a bleak existence, and when Elizabeth Gaskell, the Manchester novelist, first met Charlotte the survivor in 1850, she wrote to a friend that 'such a life as Miss B's I never heard of'.[2] Gaskell visited Charlotte in the Parsonage after the deaths of all her sisters and brother, and her vivid impression of Charlotte's loneliness coloured her imagining of the children's earlier bereavement. When, after Charlotte's own death in 1855, Gaskell wrote *The Life of Charlotte Brontë* (1857), she painted an unforgettable picture of the children's solitary friendlessness, already 'grave and silent beyond their years' and now, after the deaths of mother and elder sisters, 'quieter and lonelier still' (G. 43, 46).

More recent scholars, however, give us a different picture of their early life, and we can perhaps see why two different views were possible by looking at the 'Diary Paper' which Emily and Anne wrote in 1837, when they were in their late teens. The paper includes a sketch of the two girls sitting at a table strewn with papers (A. 486). The servants from whom Gaskell gained some of her impressions might well have seen such bookish children as 'grave and silent beyond their years', but the picture changes when you learn what they were reading and writing. Gaskell herself recognized that the children 'did not want society' because 'they were all in all to each other' (G. 46), and she reported with astonishment a quantity of tiny books, sewn into paper covers, written in minuscule script and only a few centimetres wide, which the children had written after Charlotte and Emily returned home from Cowan Bridge School.

Gaskell, anxious to get on with her biography, and able to decipher the writing only with the aid of a magnifying glass, probably read only a few of the earlier little books, and although she was impressed with their precocious range and ambition, some of their subject matter was at odds with her intention to present Charlotte not only as a writer, but as a respectable Victorian lady. When she read the stories which Charlotte was writing at the age of 13, Gaskell described them to a friend as 'the wildest & most incoherent things', which 'give one the idea of creative power carried to the verge of insanity'.[3] Nowadays we know a great deal more about the 'little books', thanks to the modern scholars who have edited the texts and analysed their contents.[4] Gaskell herself, however, quotes Charlotte's account of how some of this writing came about. In Charlotte's 'History of the Year' (1829), she describes how

> Papa bought Branwell some wooden soldiers at Leeds [and] next morning Branwell came to our door with a box of soldiers. Emily and I jumped out of bed, and I snatched up one and exclaimed, 'This is the Duke of Wellington! This shall be the Duke!' When I had said this Emily likewise took one up and said it should be hers; when Anne came down, she said one should be hers. Mine was the prettiest of the whole, and the tallest, and the most perfect in every part. (G. 70)

Christine Alexander, definitive editor of the earliest writings, points out that

> a striking feature of this early imaginative play is the confidence and bravado of the players that belies the usual story of the Brontës' desolate childhood, derived from Gaskell's account of the four motherless children huddled together against a hostile environment, living with their morose father in an isolated village on the edge of the Yorkshire Moors. (A. p. xv)

In 'The History of the Year', Charlotte certainly comes across as confident and assertive. If her enthusiasm for the Duke of Wellington seems surprising, we should remember that in 1829, not only was the Duke a military hero, victor of Waterloo (the decisive battle which took place, in 1815, only a year before Charlotte's birth), but he was currently Prime Minister, and the children knew all about him because they read the newspapers. Earlier in 'The History of the Year', Charlotte explains that

> we take two and see three newspapers a week. We take the 'Leeds Intelligencer', Tory, and the 'Leeds Mercury', Whig, edited by Mr Baines, and his brother, son-in-law, and his two sons, Edward and Talbot. We see the 'John Bull'; it is a high Tory, very violent. Mr Driver lends us it, as likewise 'Blackwood's Magazine', the most able periodical there is... (G. 69)

3

and Charlotte goes on to name the editor (with his age and birthday), and all the contributors, including 'James Hogg, a man of most extraordinary genius, a Scottish shepherd' (G. 69).[5] It is difficult to imagine a 13-year-old girl of today being so engaged with newspaper personnel, but these journalists were the media stars of their time, with the ability to rouse not just intellectual interest but also high emotion. In the Brontës' early writings, real events and people from the news evolve into fictitious characters who feature in imaginary places and events, and the two worlds are not clearly separated.

In the second volume of Charlotte's 'Tales of the Islanders', she suddenly interrupts her story about a school insurrection on an island off the coast of Africa to introduce an account of the real Parliamentary debate on the Catholic Emancipation Bill of 1829:

> Parliament was opened & the great Catholic Question was brought forward & the Duke's measures were disclosed, and all was slander, violence, party spirit & confusion. O those 3 months, from the time of the King's speech to the end! Nobody could think, speak or write on anything but the Catholic Question and the Duke of Wellington or Mr Peel. I remember the day when the Intelligence Extraordinary came with Mr Peel's speech in it, containing the terms on which the Catholics were to be let in. With what eagerness Papa tore off the cover, & how we all gathered rou[nd h]im, & with what breathless anxiety we listened, a[s o]ne by one they were disclosed & explained and argued upon so ably & so well, & then, when it was all out, how Aunt said she thought it was excellent & that the Catholics [could] do no harm with such good security. I remember also the doubts as to whether it would pass into the House of Lord[s] & the prophecies that it would not. Wh[en] the paper came which was to decide the question, the anxiety was almost dreadful with which we listen[ed] to the whole affair: the opening of the doors, the hus[h], the royal dukes in their robes & the great Duke in green sash & waistcoat, the rising of all the peeresses when he rose, the reading of his speec[h], Papa saying that his words were like precious gold &, lastly, the majority one to 4 in favour of the bill. But this is a digression.... (A. 18–19)[6]

The breathless enthusiasm with which Charlotte describes the scene suggests not only her vivid capacity for dramatic visualization, but also that she lived in an atmosphere like a domestic hothouse. Central to this shared excitement, at least at this early stage of the children's writing, was the figure of 'Papa'.

Gaskell, meeting the Reverend Patrick Brontë late in his life, was intimidated by his austere manner and misled by stories from disgruntled servants. She represented him as reclusive and eccentric. Juliet Barker, however, the author of the most authoritative modern biography of the Brontës, has uncovered a quite different view of Patrick Brontë.[7] By researching local records, she has shown his attention to national politics (writing letters to the newspapers, for instance), his close involvement in the affairs of Haworth parish and, most importantly for Charlotte as a future writer, his keen interest in his children's education. This supposedly 'morose' father even has a sense of humour, and his reaction to Gaskell's stories of his eccentricity was unexpectedly mild. In a letter to Gaskell he wrote that 'I do not deny that I am somewhat excentrick. Had I been numbered amongst the calm, sedate, *concentric* men of the world, I should not have been as I now am, and I should, in all probability, never have had such children as mine have been' (B. 947).

In their adulation of the 'Great Duke', the children are clearly responding to Papa's judgement ('his words were like precious gold'), and Papa's interpretation of the outside world must, at least in the beginning, have provided the framework of value for what they read in the newspapers. Patrick Brontë had, in fact, much to convey to his children from his own experience, which began in another century and another country. Named Patrick Prunty or Brunty, he was born in 1777, in a two-roomed cottage in Drumballyroney, County Down, in Ireland, the eldest of ten children. Amazingly, at the age of 16 he opened his own school and at 21 he was tutor in the family of Thomas Tighe, a local Wesleyan squire. Under Tighe's patronage he travelled to England, entered St John's College, Cambridge, and in 1807 was ordained priest of the Church of England in the Chapel Royal of St James, Westminster. Patrick's early life called for courage, not to endure grief, but to take risks and realize ambition. If there was a certain bravado, however, in his astonishing rise from Irish cottage to Chapel Royal, it also called for prudence.

Drumballyroney, though predominantly Protestant, had a significant Catholic minority, and Patrick's own mother may have been a Catholic. At this time the whole of Ireland was under British rule and Catholics in both countries were debarred from civic office, from voting and from sitting in

Parliament. The Church of England feared encroachment by the Church of Rome, while the British government was under threat from the Catholic majority in Ireland, who clamoured for civil rights. These incendiary pressures were forcibly brought home to Patrick when, in 1798, one of his brothers took part in the armed rebellion of United Irishmen, inspired and supported by French Revolutionary forces, and attempting, among other things, to win civil rights for Catholics. The scenes of violence which Patrick then experienced in the very area where he was living in Thomas Tighe's Protestant household, and the British army's punitive massacres of defeated rebels, produced a life-long horror of insurrection, and help to explain his curiously liberal conservatism, which Charlotte came to share. Each of them combines sympathy for the oppressed with a fervent belief in the rule of law. Hence came his heart-felt relief at the Catholic Emancipation Bill of 1829, which granted the rights which he hoped would defuse further explosions.[8]

The Catholics were not the only threat to the peace in Patrick's youth. In 1802, when he travelled to England, he found there not only alarm at events in Ireland but also an atmosphere of fierce and fearful antipathy to the violence of the French Revolution and the aggression of Napoleon Bonaparte. England had been at war with Revolutionary France since 1793, and would continue at war with Napoleon until 1815. In this climate, Patrick aligned himself with the forces of law and order. On arrival in Cambridge he registered his name as 'Brontë', in homage to Lord Nelson, hero of the Battle of the Nile (1798) and newly created 'Duke of Brontë' by a grateful King of Naples. In 1804 he joined a body of volunteers mustered to oppose a French invasion, proudly serving under the command of the young Lord Palmerston, who soon became Secretary at War. In the same spirit he eagerly followed the Peninsular campaigns (1807–14) under the command of Arthur Wellesley, later the Duke of Wellington. The names of Wellesley's victories at Talavera, Salamanca and Vittoria were well known to the Brontë children, and appear in their early writing.

Overseas wars, however, were not the end of Patrick's encounters with his turbulent times. After his ordination in 1807 he took up curacies in Essex, Shropshire and finally in the woollen-processing towns of west Yorkshire. Here he encountered at close range the acute poverty and squalid living conditions of the new urban working class created by the industrial revolution, which was replacing hand-loom work with large-scale machinery, making workers redundant in an era when unemployment meant starvation. Conditions became even worse when, as part of the campaign against Napoleon, the government issued 'Orders in Council' restricting trade with France by neutral countries, including the United States, which was a major customer for Yorkshire wool. In retaliation, America withheld orders from British firms, trade fell to disastrous levels and the workers in desperation began a campaign of machine-breaking led by the mythical 'Captain Ludd'. In 1811 there were more government troops fighting the Luddites than there were in the Peninsular War, and Patrick found himself once more in the midst of this trouble. In 1812, he was curate at Hartshead, where men from his parish joined in Luddite attacks on machinery in transit and, famously, on Rawfold's Mill. Patrick deplored the violence but stories of industrial insurrection, undoubtedly derived from his experience, appear not only in the children's early tales but also in Charlotte's mature novel, *Shirley* (1849).

Although the young Brontës took their lead from their father's outlook, their early writing was not slavishly conformist. The tiny size of their books, probably chosen to fit the toy soldiers, was also a kind of security against adult interference. Elizabeth Gaskell, as we have seen, was clearly shocked by some of what she read. She sees 'singular merit' in some of Charlotte's stories, but 'while her description of any real occurrence is ... homely, graphic, and forcible', she writes, 'when she gives way to her powers of creation, her fancy and her language alike run riot, sometimes to the very borders of apparent delirium' (G. 67, 71).

This variety of style derived partly from the young Brontës' favourite journal, *Blackwood's Edinburgh Magazine*, which included Gothic and supernatural tales as well as sober accounts of politics, science and exploration. *Blackwood's* also provided a stable format for their writing, since they copied its structure even to the setting-out of their title pages and imagined publication details. They also learned the different rhetorical skills appropriate to its various *genres* of writing – 'stories, articles, poems, reviews of paintings and books, letters to the editor, and "Conversations", the latter based on the renowned discussions of literary and current affairs known as "Noctes Ambrosianae"' (A. p. xix). The variety of *genres* called for a multiplicity of voices, and both Charlotte and Branwell developed many clearly-distinguished personae.

It is interesting, for instance, to see how Charlotte re-writes the episode of the toy soldiers for a different voice. In 'The History of the Year', she and her siblings appear as themselves, and it is Charlotte who claims one of the twelve soldiers to be 'the Duke of Wellington'. Her story called 'The Twelve Adventurers', however, is written from the point of view of the 'twelve' themselves, including the young Arthur Wellesley (who, historically, would become the Duke of Wellington). In the story, the twelve set off from England by ship and are blown off course to Trinidad and then to west Africa, where they build the great city of Glass Town. In response to supernatural summons, they trek for a day and a night through a vast desert, where they find 'a palace of diamond, the pillars of which were ruby and emerald, illuminated with lamps too bright to look upon'. This is the home of 'the Princes of the Genii', who sit on thrones surrounded by genii and fairies 'whose robes were of beaten gold sparkling with diamonds'. One of the chief Genii seizes Arthur Wellesley and exclaims '"This is the Duke of Wellington"'. She (it is, of course, Charlotte) then foretells the future duke's glorious career (A. 11). The change of perspective takes a 'real' event (the arrival of the toy soldiers) and allows it to be elaborated into a tale of travel, magic and a transformed version of history. The creative force of narrative confers on the mundane children of the Parsonage a supernatural power.

A different change of focus occurs in 'Tales of the Islanders' (1829) where the Duke, now an elder statesman, tells his two sons of a vision which he experienced in Salamanca, during the Peninsular Wars. The vision foretells his future encounter with 'a tremendous monster...black & hideous.... He was clothed in the skin of wild beasts & in his forehead was branded...the word "bigotry"'. In the vision, the Duke overcomes the monster by flinging at him 'a dart on which the word "justice" was written in golden characters' (A. 26). The dart is, of course, the Emancipation Bill, expressed in the form of an allegory. The variety of styles employed in even these two examples shows that Charlotte was drawing on a range of sources apart from *Blackwood's*: the Bible's Book of Revelation (for the gem-studded palace), the *Arabian Nights' Entertainment* (for the genii) and Bunyan's *Pilgrim's Progress* (for the monster), and the children's later writings are remarkable for their range of allusion, including Scott, Shakespeare and classical sources.

The toy soldiers were, of course, all men. Branwell's was at first Napoleon (a fitting adversary for Charlotte's Duke of Wellington) and later evolved into Alexander Percy, Earl of Northangerland. Emily and Anne chose Parry and Ross, British naval heroes whose Arctic explorations were reported in *Blackwood's*. In their invented countries of Glass Town (later 'Verdopolis') and Angria, as in the real world, it was men who sailed oceans, settled colonies, built cities and fought battles. As Charlotte grew into her teens, however, her notion of masculine heroism was transformed by the poetry of Byron.

The famous novels by Charlotte, Emily and Anne were published in the 1840s and 1850s, during the Victorian era which we associate with sexual prudery and social convention. Their father, however, grew up in the eighteenth century, and the children themselves were growing up in the pre-Victorian period which is loosely thought of as the 'Regency'. The Prince Regent, who became George IV in 1820, gave his name to the style of extravagant, aristocratic excess, both frivolous and ostentatious, which is described in the so-called 'silver fork' novels of the period, and which persisted until the rule of Victoria began in 1837.[9] The future queen, who was just the same age as Emily, did indeed have a most decorous upbringing, but in Charlotte's 'Tales of the Islanders' (1829) 'Princess Vittoria' appears as an unruly schoolgirl, 'constantly quarrelling & fighting...in a most outrageous manner' and currently 'encamped in a very wild part of the island' (A. 20–1).

One result of this pre-Victorian context was that Patrick Brontë did not exercise the moral censorship thought appropriate for girls later in the century. Even in the 1820s, it was still remarkable that he allowed his daughters to read not just the newspapers but the poetry of Byron, who, though 'controversial', was 'still hugely popular'[10] among a fashionable elite, although in more sober circles he appeared scandalous and immoral. Robert Southey, for instance, who was Poet Laureate from 1813, and to whom Charlotte would later appeal for advice, regarded Byron's *Don Juan* as 'a high crime…against society', mingling mockery with 'horrors, filth with impiety, profligacy with sedition and slander'.[11] In her late teens, Charlotte Brontë aligned herself with fashion rather than piety, devouring the works of Byron with a relish, according to Christine Alexander, 'bordering on obsession'.[12] Byron's heroes, in *Childe Harold's Pilgrimage* (1812–18) and in his 'Turkish Tales' – 'The Giaour', 'The Bride of Abydos', 'The Corsair' and 'Lara' (1813–14) – were still adventurers, pirates and soldiers, but their temperament was more fascinating than anything Charlotte had met so far. They were handsome, brave, imperious, sardonic, moody, mysterious and irresistible to women. By 1834, when Charlotte was 18, she had also read Moore's *Life of Byron* (1830) and knew all about Byron's marriage, his infidelities, his incestuous love for his half-sister and his illegitimate daughter whose mother was Mary Shelley's step-sister. By now, Charlotte's fictional handling of the Duke of Wellington had become respectful but rather bland, and her focus turned to his two sons. The elder, also called Arthur Wellesley, Marquis of Douro, evolved into the Glass Town aristocrat the Duke of Zamorna, who became the King of Angria. Zamorna was Byronic in every way, beginning like a young god, but transforming through the saga into a cynical and ambitious character, ruthless in his relations with women.

The Byronic model of romance was thrilling from a masculine viewpoint, but gave Charlotte no escape from the sense that women, even heroines, were helpless pawns in men's world, with at best a masochistic kind of recompense. In 'The Spell' (1834), we encounter Mina Laury, Zamorna's mistress and nurse/governess to his children. A low-born subject, she relishes her subjection, proud to be 'his born thrall'. Zamorna's doctor describes her as 'the doomed slave of infatuation – devoted, stricken, absorbed in one idea, finding a kind of strange pleasure in bearing the burden & carrying the yoke of him whose fascination fettered her so strongly' (A. 114). Such women are the natural complement to the Byronic hero, and all the women linked to Zamorna – even his three aristocratic wives – are 'in thrall' to his fascination.[13]

Charlotte did have a weapon against overweening masculinity, and this was irony. Despite indulging in what Fannie Ratchford called 'an orgy of Byronism'[14] in her portrayal of Zamorna, Charlotte was able to keep a certain distance from her creation by means of her second persona, Zamorna's younger brother, Lord Charles Wellesley, who is consistently flippant, insubordinate and sarcastic, especially at the expense of his lordly brother. The most complete portrait we have of Zamorna comes, in fact, through the words of this sniping brother, as he takes 'A Peep into a Picture Book' (written by Charlotte in 1834):

> Fire and Light! What have we here? Zamorna's self, blazing in the frontispiece like the sun on his own standard!...All his usual insufferableness or irresistibleness, or whatever the ladies choose to call it, surrounding him like an atmosphere, he stands as if a thunderbolt could neither blast the light of his eyes nor dash the effrontery of his brow. Keen, glorious being!...Oh, Zamorna! What eyes those are glancing under the deep shadow of that raven crest! They bode no good....All here is passion and fire unquenchable. Impetuous sin, stormy pride, diving and soaring enthusiasm, war and poetry are kindling their fires in all his veins, and his wild blood boils from his heart and back again like a torrent of new-sprung lava. Young duke – Young demon![15]

Byron himself, of course, wrote self-mockingly in *Don Juan* (1819–24), and Charlotte was also familiar with the ironic tone of the fashionable novels of her Regency youth.

Heather Glen demonstrates convincingly that the social milieu of Charlotte's 1830s writing derives from 'silver fork' novels such as Edward Bulwer-Lytton's *Pelham* (1828), which were reviewed and extracted in *Blackwood's*. In Charlotte's tales, Glen argues,

> as in silver fork fiction, the reader is given a half-ironic, half-fascinated portrait of a privileged beau monde. There is the same emphasis on talk – scandal, 'fashionable intelligence' (or society news), political rumours, newspaper reports, drawing-room repartee; the same cast of characters – roués, society belles, hard-up younger brothers and sought-after parvenue heiresses; the same aristocratic 'slang' and fashionable sprinkling of French. Here, also, the dandy is a prominent figure.[16]

It is, of course, the dandy Charles Wellesley, later appearing as Charles Townshend, whose sardonic viewpoint colours Charlotte's later Angrian tales, and readers who are only familiar with her published work may well be astonished at the jaunty, dissipated tone and racy, man-about-town slang of novelettes like 'Stancliffe's Hotel' (1838) and 'Henry Hastings' (1839).[17] 'Henry Hastings' begins with Townshend's advertisement for a wife; he is not, he writes, too particular about 'an eye too few or a row of teeth minus... provided only satisfactory testimonials be given of the possession of that one great and paramount virtue, that eminent and irresistible charm, C-A-S-H!' This advertisement, he tells the reader, is

> the last resource of an unoffending and meritorious individual who, penniless and placeless, found himself driven upon the two horns of a hideous dilemma, and – all other attempts to raise the wind by less desperate methods having failed – compelled either to write or to wed. For the last six months I have been living, as it were, on turtle-soup and *foie gras*. I have been rowing and revelling and rioting to my heart's content, but now, alas, my pockets are empty and my pleasures are gone. I must either write a book or marry a wife, to refill the one and to recall the other.[18]

Irony, however, depends on a knowing audience, and did not serve Charlotte so well in the real world. By 1834, when, as Charles Wellesley, she wrote 'A Peep into a Picture Book', her intimacy with Branwell and the others had already been broken when, for about eighteen months in 1831–2, Charlotte went away to school – this time, to Roe Head School, Mirfield, an entirely satisfactory establishment run by Miss Margaret Wooler, who became Charlotte's lifelong friend. The school was comfortable and home-like, with only eight or nine pupils, and offered genuine education, including French and drawing. Perhaps more important, it introduced Charlotte to people outside Haworth and outside the Parsonage. Two fellow-pupils in particular became her friends and invited her to their homes: Mary Taylor, whose family was the model for the Yorke family in *Shirley*, and Ellen Nussey, who became Charlotte's particular confidante. These two girls were very different in temperament and opinions, Mary being extrovert and radical, while Ellen was decorous and conservative. In 1845 Mary took the extraordinary step of emigrating to New Zealand (then truly a frontier community) and setting up shop, and it is to be regretted that she kept only one of Charlotte's letters, since Charlotte wrote in a less guarded way to Mary than to the more easily-shocked

Ellen. It is to Ellen, however, that we owe much of what we know of Charlotte's life, since she kept the hundreds of letters which Charlotte wrote to her over more than twenty years, and allowed Elizabeth Gaskell to weave them into her *Life*.

In 1835, after three more years at home, Charlotte returned to Roe Head as a teacher, and for short periods first Emily and then Anne went with her as pupils, their fees being paid by Charlotte's work. Although Charlotte had relished the opportunity to learn, she was miserable as a teacher. Her pupils, unlike her precocious brother and sisters, had no intellectual curiosity, and as a teacher she had little contact with her sisters even while they were at school. Above all, Charlotte felt isolated from the imaginative play, the jokes, parodies and allusions which had fed the endlessly fascinating developments of their shared invented worlds. Even if she were at home, Emily and Anne had already split off from the Glass Town/Angrian saga to form their own fictional country of Gondal, and Branwell, preoccupied with battles, was impatient with Charlotte's intrigues and love stories. Moreover, she became more and more conscious of her difference from other young women, who seemed, like Ellen, to live calmly in the way society expected, while she felt her daily life mostly as an interruption to the world of her imagination. As a parson's daughter, she was also aware that the increasingly sexual nature of her imaginings was probably sinful, and this was reinforced by conversations with the sedately pious Ellen. In a letter of 1836 she writes: 'Don't deceive yourself by imagining that I have a bit of real goodness about me. . . . I am *not like you*. If you knew my thoughts; the dreams that absorb me; and the fiery imagination that at times eats me up and makes me feel Society as it is, wretchedly insipid you would pity and I dare say despise me' (*L*. i. 144).

Charlotte's well-known poem about her imaginary world, 'We wove a web in childhood' (1835), looks back at her first term as a teacher at Roe Head. It is usually quoted in the form of short extracts which give a positive reading:

> We wove a web in childhood,
> A web of sunny air;
> We dug a spring in infancy
> Of water pure and fair.

> We sowed in youth a mustard seed,
> We cut an almond rod;
> We are now grown up to riper age –
> Are they withered in the sod?
>
> .   .   .   .
>
> The mustard-seed on distant land
> Bends down a mighty tree,
> The dry unbudded almond-wand
> Has touched eternity. (A. 151)

In its entirety, however, this is a poem of several pages which goes on to define her desperate need of that other world:

> When I sat 'neath a strange roof-tree
> With naught I knew or loved around me,
> Oh how my heart shrank back to thee –
> Then I felt how fast thy tie had bound me. (A. 152)

Her desolate state is only relieved when 'that bright, darling dream' carries her away in thought, first to her 'moorland home' and then rapidly on until 'in one short hour a hundred homes/ Had roofed me with their lordly domes' (A. 153). A particular story, focussed on the 'demi-god' Zamorna, now develops and after another two pages the urgency of the story turns to prose.

> Never shall I, Charlotte Brontë, forget what a voice of wild & wailing music now came thrillingly to my mind's – almost to my body's – ear; nor how distinctly I, sitting in the schoolroom at Roe Head, saw the Duke of Zamorna leaning against that obelisk, with the mute marble Victory above him, the fern waving at his feet, his black horse turned loose grazing among the heather, the moonlight so mild & so exquisitely tranquil, sleeping upon that vast & vacant road, & the African sky quivering & shaking with stars expanded above all. I was quite gone. I had really utterly forgot where I was and all the gloom & cheerlessness of my situation. I felt myself breathing quick and short as I beheld the Duke lifting up his sable crest, which undulated as the plume of a hearse waves to the wind, & knew that the music ... was exciting him & quickening his ever rapid pulse.

> 'Miss Brontë, what are you thinking about?' said a voice that dissipated all the charm, & Miss Lister thrust her little, rough black head into my face! 'Sic transit' &c. (A. 156–7)

Here, writing in her own voice, she presents the attractions of Zamorna without irony, and in the fragments of writing known as the 'Roe Head Journal', written during the next two years (183–7), Charlotte continued in this painfully divided state between reality and a drug-like dream. It is important to remember that although the Brontës' early writings are often called their 'juvenilia', Charlotte was 23 when she left Roe Head and much of this writing is far from juvenile. The balance between her actual life and what she and Branwell came to call 'the infernal world' (A. 162) is dangerously weighted towards unreality because the 'real' world offers her so little. The Duke of Wellington, the Duke of Zamorna – even 'Papa' – might find space in their lives for 'bravado', and as a child she could speak with their voices and join in their adventures, but as a young woman, she was learning, she needed only 'courage to endure':

> The thought came over me: am I to spend all the best part of my life in this wretched bondage, forcibly suppressing my rage at the idleness, the apathy and the hyperbolical & most asinine stupidity of those fat-headed oafs, and on compulsion assuming an air of kindness, patience & asiduity? Must I from day to day sit chained to this chair, prisoned with in these four bare walls, while these glorious summer suns are burning in heaven & the year is revolving in its richest glow & declaring at the close of every summer day [that] the time I am losing will never come again? (A. 162)

Flinging open the window, she hears distant church bells.

> Then came on me, rushing impetuously, all the mighty phantasm that we had conjured from nothing to a system strong as some religious creed. I felt as if I could have written gloriously – I longed to write. The spirit of all Verdopolis, of all the mountainous North, of all the woodland West, of all the river-watered East came crowding into my mind. If I had had time to indulge it, I felt that the vague sensations of that moment would have settled down into some narrative better at least than any thing I ever produced before. But just then a dolt came up with a lesson. I thought I should have vomited. (A. 163)

The real world not only failed to give her scope for her talents, it also offered a dearth of fascinating men. In 1839, after finally leaving Miss Wooler's school, Charlotte refused two unsatisfactory proposals of marriage, writing to Ellen's brother Henry that

> I am not the serious, grave, cool-headed individual you suppose –

15

you would think me romantic and [eccentric – you would] say I was satirical and [severe – however I scorn] deceit and I will never for the sake of attaining the distinction of matrimony and escaping the stigma of an old maid take a worthy man whom I am conscious I cannot render happy. (*L. i.* 185)

Charlotte knew that marriage was regarded as what one of Jane Austen's characters calls a woman's 'pleasantest preservative from want',[19] but she also knew that she would not settle for mere comfort. With this attitude, and what she pointedly refers to in this letter as her lack of '"*personal attractions*"', her future life, like that of her sisters, was destined to be dull and laborious, lacking even the glamour of thralldom. Her father had no fortune to leave her and even their parsonage home would be lost when he died. She must work for a living, and if she could not succeed as a teacher in a school then she must become a governess in a private house.

As she travelled to take up her first post in the imposing home of Mrs Sidgwick, of Stonegappe, near Skipton, she felt a certain excitement at the idea of seeing silver fork life at first hand, but the promise was hollow, and she survived only three months. To Emily she wrote, 'I used to think I should like to be in the stir of grand folks' society but I have had enough of it – it is dreary work to look on and listen. I see now more clearly than I have ever done before that a private governess has no existence, is not considered as a living and rational being except as connected with the wearisome duties she has to fulfil' (*L. i.* 191).

Escaping the Sidgwicks, she began to write 'Caroline Vernon' (1839), her longest work of fiction so far and the last to be generally included in her 'juvenilia'. Its heroine is more lively and individual than Zamorna's previous victims, but although Caroline fervently admires active men, and scorns 'a common place' or a 'dull droning life' (A. 256, 266), her idea of an 'unhackneyed' existence is still 'to die for somebody she loves' (A. 268) and she too yields to Zamorna 'with a kind of wild devoted enthusiasm' (A. 308). Because this story is narrated by Charles Townshend, both Caroline's infatuation and Zamorna's egotism are subject to his usual irony, producing what Heather Glen calls 'a disconcerting sense of the absurdity of rampant masculinity', epitomized by 'the exaggerated braggadocio of the final confrontation between Zamorna and Northangerland'.[20]

16

Glen goes so far as to say that '"hero worship" ... is emphatically, ironically absent from these last of Charlotte's Angrian tales'.[21]

There is, however, nothing satisfying about the abrupt ending to this tale, in which Caroline – the girl who started out so 'original and peculiar' (A. 258) – disappears from the story, which remains focussed on the two powerful men who can claim to 'possess' her – her lover Zamorna and her natural father, Northangerland. 'Bravado' may be exposed as 'braggadocio', as Glen argues, but in the story, as in the real world, irony cannot disguise the fact that Caroline has come to a bad end and it is the men who have scope for action. Charlotte needed not just to deflate but to escape from Zamorna's spell, and while still writing 'Caroline Vernon' she wrote her 'Farewell to Angria'. 'I long to quit for a while that burning clime', she writes, 'where we have sojourned too long. Its skies flame – the glow of sunset is always upon it. The mind would cease from excitement & turn now to a cooler region, where the dawn breaks grey and sober & the coming day for a time at least is subdued in clouds' (A. 314).

Branwell never abandoned Angria, and Emily was writing Gondal poems until she died. Anne, who endured six years of governessing, wearied of Gondal and began her first published novel resolutely: 'All true histories contain instruction'.[22] Charlotte, however, felt 'agonized' without her other world to fill 'the craving vacancy' of everyday life (A. 166). In her 'Farewell' she writes, 'it is no easy thing to dismiss from my imagination the images which have filled it so long. They were my friends & my intimate acquaintance.... When I depart from these I feel almost as if I stood on the threshold of a home & were bidding farewell to its inmates'. Without it, her future life seems like 'a distant country where every face was unknown & the character of all the population an enigma which it would take much study to comprehend & much talent to expound' (A. 314). As she faced this unknown world, she might well have whispered to herself, 'Take courage, Charlotte; take courage'.

17

2

The Professor

When Charlotte Brontë, aged 23, said farewell to the 'burning
clime' of Angria which had fed her imagination for so many
years, the alternative before her was indeed 'cool', 'sober' and
'subdued' (A. 314): it was to go once again as a governess.
Writing two years later to Ellen Nussey from a post with the
White family at Upperwood House, near Bradford, she laments
that

> no one but myself can tell how hard a governess's work is to me ...
> Some of my greatest difficulties lie in things that would appear to
> you comparatively trivial....I find it so difficult to ask either servants
> or mistress for anything I want, however much I want it. It is less
> pain to me to endure the greatest inconvenience than to go [into the
> kitchen to] request its removal. (*L.* i. 246–7)

Charlotte's own character – shy, proud and not easily drawn to
children – was certainly not suited to the part of governess, but
some of her distress was inherent in the role itself, and derived
from what modern sociologists call 'status incongruence' in a
society much more rigidly controlled than ours in class terms.
The Victorian writer Elizabeth Sewell explains that 'the real
discomfort of a governess's position in a private family arises
from the fact that it is undefined. She is not a relation, not a
guest, not a mistress, not a servant – but something made up of
all. No one knows exactly how to treat her'.[1] Elizabeth Rigby
(later Lady Eastlake), writes from the employer's perspective:
'the real definition of a governess, in the English sense, is a
being who is our equal in birth, manners, and education, but our
inferior in worldly wealth. Take a lady, in every meaning of the

word, born and bred, and let her father pass through the gazette [bankruptcy], and she wants nothing more to suit our highest *beau idéal* of a guide and instructress to our children'.[2] The result, as Rigby succinctly puts it, is that 'there is no other class which so cruelly requires its members to be, in birth, mind, and manners, above their station, in order to fit them for their station'.[3]

Anne Brontë, who endured this incongruity for much longer than Charlotte, gives us an account of its indignities in *Agnes Grey* (1847), but this novel also shows that the governess's liminal position between classes was a unique vantage point for observation. The Marxist critic Terry Eagleton goes further, arguing that it is the indignation produced by status incongruence which gives the Brontës their peculiar power. Using the psychoanalytic term 'overdetermination', he argues that just as the symptoms of mental illness are the result of many causes overlapping, so the striking effects of their writing result from 'condensing into complex unity an accumulated host of subsidiary conflicts':

> They were, to begin with, placed at a painfully ambiguous point in the social structure, as the daughters of a clergyman with the inferior status of 'perpetual curate' who had thrust his way up from poverty ...They were, moreover, socially insecure *women* – members of a cruelly oppressed group whose victimised condition reflected a more widespread exploitation. And they were *educated* women, trapped in an almost intolerable deadlock between culture and economics – between imaginative aspiration and the cold truth of a society which could use them merely as 'higher' servants. They were *isolated* educated women, socially and geographically remote from a world with which they nonetheless maintained close intellectual touch, and so driven back on themselves in solitary emotional hungering.[4]

Eagleton sees this overdetermined set of pressures acting like a dynamo propelling the sisters, like their father, into upward social mobility, and indeed the next event in Charlotte's life required not endurance but bold enterprise. Despairing of the governess role, Charlotte, Emily and Anne conceived the plan of opening a school of their own. Aunt Branwell responded to their appeal for funds, and as a first step, in 1842, Charlotte and Emily embarked for Brussels, where they hoped to perfect their

French and acquire some German – essential requisites for genteel young ladies' seminaries. The two years which Charlotte spent in Brussels were the most important of her life, and furnished, in different ways, material for each of her published novels. She and Emily were established in a girls' school, the Pensionnat Heger, where the headmistress, Madame Heger, employed both resident female teachers and visiting masters, including her husband. M. Heger gave regular lessons to the older classes at the Pensionnat, and quickly recognized the unusual potential of the two young Englishwomen who were, of course, well above the usual age for schoolgirls.

M. Heger was an inventive and inspiring teacher, who set the two sisters exercises in writing in imitation of various models of French excellence, which Emily resented, as encroaching on her individuality, but which Charlotte relished. These *devoirs*, or composition exercises, survive, and thanks to Sue Lonoff's edition we can see a transcription of what they wrote, a translation into English, and M. Heger's marginal comments.[5] He evidently took great pains with them, and Charlotte responded with vigour. For the first time in her life, an authoritative, intelligent, well-educated, lively mind, outside her own family, was engaging with her own and recognizing her talent. She worked with a will, and for the first year was very happy.

Gradually the atmosphere darkened. Back in Haworth, Patrick's popular young curate, William Weightman, died of cholera. Worse still, nearby in Brussels, the cholera took Mary Taylor's vivacious young sister, Martha. Finally the death of Aunt Branwell called the sisters home, and Emily declared that she would not go back. Charlotte, drawn by her attraction to M. Heger, braved the return journey alone, but this second year was not like the first. Mme and M. Heger, growing uncomfortable with Charlotte's marked devotion to her master, withdrew their attention and left her very lonely. Effectively frozen out, she returned to Haworth early in 1844. During the next two years she wrote increasingly desperate letters, to which M. Heger did not reply.

Advertisement and enquiry, moreover, had produced no pupils for the proposed Brontë school and the plan was given up. Charlotte's little leap of enterprise had come to nothing, and endurance seemed once again her lot. Mary Taylor, by contrast, refused to 'suffer and be still'[6] and, as Charlotte wrote to Emily, 'has made up her mind she can not and will not be a governess, a teacher, a milliner, a bonnet-maker nor housemaid. She sees no means of obtaining employment she would like in England, so she is leaving it' (*L*. i. 251). In March, 1845, Mary emigrated to New Zealand, and Charlotte wrote that 'to me it is something as if a great planet fell out of the sky' (*L*. i. 372).

A heavier blow fell in the summer when first Anne and then Branwell returned home from Thorp Green Hall, near York, where they had been governess and tutor in the Robinson family. Although Anne was much valued, Branwell had been dismissed by Mr Robinson, who 'had discovered ... proceedings which he characterised as bad beyond expression': it seems that Branwell had had an affair with Mrs Robinson. Charlotte, silently enduring her hopeless love for M. Heger, had no patience with Branwell's histrionic grief at being parted from his Lydia, especially as he seemed to think 'of nothing but stunning, or drowning his distress' by opium and alcohol (*L*. i. 412). Six months later, 'the faculty of self-government' was, she wrote, 'almost destroyed in him' (*L*. i. 448).

Despite his emotional prostration, Branwell still managed not only to write but to get some of his poems placed in local newspapers, and he also made efforts at wider publication (B. 558–61). Patrick Brontë himself, as a young man, had published both poetry and prose fiction of a pious and edifying kind,[7] and both Branwell and Charlotte had already tried to make literary contacts. As early as 1836, Charlotte had sent verses to Robert Southey, the Poet Laureate, receiving the reply which feminist critics were later to make famous: that although she possessed 'the faculty of verse', 'literature cannot be the business of a woman's life, & it ought not to be' (*L*. 166–7). In 1840, she sent the opening of a novel to Hartley Coleridge. His answer is lost but we do have a draft of her response (probably never sent), in which she mocks herself for having written from a state in which 'the ideal and the actual are no longer distinct notions in your mind but amalgamate in an interesting medley from whence result looks, thoughts and manners bordering on the idiotic' (*L*. i. 236). Even in this miserable year of 1845, however, she was still writing.

Suddenly, a ray of light appeared. 'One day, in the autumn of 1845', she writes,

I accidentally lighted on a MS. volume of verse in my sister Emily's handwriting. Of course, I was not surprised, knowing that she could and did write verse: I looked it over, and something more than surprise seized me, – a deep conviction that these were not common effusions, nor at all like the poetry women generally write. I thought them condensed and terse, vigorous and genuine. To my ear, they had also a peculiar music – wild, melancholy, and elevating.[8]

Charlotte's 'deep conviction' gave her the energy to overcome Emily's rooted reluctance to publish this work. 'We had', Charlotte writes, 'very early cherished the dream of one day becoming authors. This dream...now suddenly acquired strength and consistency: it took the character of a resolve'.[9] After days of persuasion, Emily agreed to add her poems to those already written by Charlotte and Anne, and Charlotte organized publication, at their own expense, with the little-known firm of Aylott & Jones. One of Emily's conditions was that the publication be pseudonymous, and the book appeared as *Poems by Currer, Ellis, and Acton Bell*, 'the ambiguous choice' of names, Charlotte explains, 'being dictated by a sort of conscientious scruple at assuming Christian names positively masculine, while we did not like to declare ourselves women, because ... we had a vague impression that authoresses are liable to be looked on with prejudice'.[10] A year later only two copies had been sold, but the review copies which were widely distributed yielded three positive reviews. *The Critic* was particularly pleased, writing that 'here we have good, wholesome, refreshing, vigorous poetry...original thoughts, expressed in the true language of poetry'.[11]

Charlotte was under no illusion about her own verse, and Tom Winnifrith, her modern editor, writes bluntly that 'Charlotte was probably the worst poet in the family after her father'. Certainly, as he argues, Charlotte's poems 'cannot stand up to the stark contrast with Emily's',[12] but they do show what Southey had called 'the faculty of verse'. Written mostly in rhymed iambic tetrameter (a four-stressed line) or in ballad meter (alternating four- and three-stressed lines), they use a narrative form to explore emotional states, and display skill in varying the pace, the stanza form and rhyme scheme and in choosing words for emotional effect. Although many of these poems were written before her stay in Brussels, they share an atmosphere of frustration, betrayal and loneliness into which her Belgian experience fitted only too easily. In a pair of poems almost certainly written in 1843, Charlotte first speaks as 'Frances', an abandoned lover, and then from the point of view of 'Gilbert', a careless betrayer. Frances bears 'the yoke of absolute despair', since 'unloved – I love; unwept – I weep':

> For me the universe is dumb,
> Stone-deaf, and blank, and wholly blind;
> Life I must bound, existence sum
> In the strait limits of one mind;[13]

Gilbert, by contrast, reflects complacently on the 'despot-might' which gave him power over the 'trembling eagerness' of the woman – not his wife – who loved him. The melodramatic force of this poem lies in Gilbert's vision, while sitting by his own safe fireside, of a sea-storm showing him a drowned woman, whose ghost eventually drives him to suicide, heeding 'Heaven's stern but just decree:/''The measure thou to her didst mete,/To thee shall measured be!'''.[14] While 'Frances' seems deeply felt, 'Gilbert' relies on Gothic effects and an unpleasantly vindictive denouement. Charlotte herself later wrote that 'I do not like my own share of the work ... the restless effervescence of a mind that would not be still. In those days, the sea too often "wrought and was tempestuous", and weed, sand, shingle – all turned up in the tumult' (L. ii. 475).

A theme from further back in Charlotte's life is the woman chafing at inaction. In 'The Wife's Will' and 'The Wood', a wife sees happiness in sharing her husband's dangers, with 'all my once waste energy/To weighty purpose bent'.[15] This need for action and for 'weighty purpose' in Charlotte's own life seems to have been answered by their publishing venture, despite its muted success, and she was eager for further enterprise. The poems appeared in May, 1846, and by June of that year she was writing to enquire about the publication of 'three tales' – Charlotte's *The Professor*, Emily's *Wuthering Heights* and Anne's *Agnes Grey*.

The reason for offering the three works together was that the Victorian fiction-publishing market was dominated by circulating libraries, especially Mudie's and W. H. Smith's, and they preferred novels in three volumes which could be lent out one volume at a time. None of the three 'tales' which the sisters had completed would make three volumes by itself, but they hoped to exploit the fashion by offering them together. Now began a tedious process. Charlotte packed up the three manuscripts and sent them to one publisher after another. Eventually Thomas Newby agreed to take *Wuthering Heights* and *Agnes Grey*, but not *The Professor*. It was rejected nine times in all and was never published in Charlotte's lifetime. It is, however, worth our attention.

The 'Preface' which is now printed with *The Professor* was not written at the same time as the novel, but after the publication of *Shirley*, when Charlotte made a last attempt to interest Smith, Elder in its publication. The Preface does, however, look back to the original time of writing, explaining (with some irony in view of the reception of the novel) that her aim had been to achieve the goal expressed in her 'Farewell to Angria', to write about what was 'sober' and 'subdued':

> I had got over any such taste as I might once have had for the ornamented and redundant in composition – and had come to prefer what was plain and homely. . . . I said to myself that my hero should work his way through life as I had seen real living men work theirs – that he should never get a shilling he had not earned – that no sudden turns should lift him in a moment to wealth and high station – that whatever small competency he might gain should be won by the sweat of his brow . . . that he should not even marry a beautiful nor a rich wife, nor a lady of rank – As Adam's Son he should share Adam's doom – Labour throughout life and a mixed and moderate cup of enjoyment. (*P.* 3)

This resolve meant taming not only the highly coloured Angrian style but also the emotional potential of her Brussels experience. And yet *The Professor* is set in Brussels. As Tom Winnifrith once said in a lecture, Charlotte fell in love with a married Belgian teacher: can it be a coincidence that each of her heroes is either married, Belgian, a teacher, or a combination of these? Yet to make this point is not to read the work as simple autobiography. What is remarkable here, as in her early writing, is the extent to which Charlotte can rework similar material from different standpoints.

In the first place, although *The Professor* has a first-person narrator, that person is not Charlotte, or even a woman. As in Angria, so in the 'sober' world of reality, it was the men who had scope for action. In announcing that 'my hero should work his way through life', Charlotte is adopting the newly popular form of the Bildungsroman, or novel of personal development, and as feminist critics note, even much later in the nineteenth century the life story which for male characters was a 'voyage out' from childhood to social standing, was for women more usually a 'voyage in', in which physical maturity led back into the domestic world of childhood, or to what Eagleton calls 'solitary emotional hungering'.[16] *The Professor*, by contrast, is an exemplary 'voyage out', written in the social atmosphere which culminated in Samuel Smiles's *Self-Help* (1859). Heather Glen points out that 'the lectures that formed the basis of Smiles's best-seller...were first delivered to a young men's mutual improvement society in Leeds in 1845 – the year in which, very probably, only a few miles away, *The Professor* was conceived'.[17]

William Crimsworth, the hero of *The Professor*, does indeed 'work his way', but it is notable that he is not, like Patrick Brontë, of humble origin; he has the advantages of aristocratic birth and an Eton education. Like Dickens's David Copperfield (1850), he resents his lowly position partly because he expected something better. In this, however, he is also characteristic of his age. The England which Patrick Brontë encountered in 1802 was governed by men whose power derived from land, and whose younger sons, who did not inherit the land, could be placed in respectable professions – the church, the army or the law. By the 1840s, the industrial revolution had thrown up a class of wealthy entrepreneurs whose power lay in the ownership of factories and the capital to work them. In this environment, those unendowed by the aristocratic system, like William's brother Edward, could rise to greater heights, but in a world which Heather Glen describes as one of 'ominous instability', they could also, like William, fall.[18]

William's history, as one of two hostile brothers disowned by aristocratic relatives, originates in Angria, and the two-brother motif seems to have fascinated Charlotte.[19] William's position as a disadvantaged younger brother invites response on several planes: it is socially realistic, but it is also a fairy-tale motif, while his consciousness of being 'kept-down – like some desolate tutor or governess' (*P.* 20) mimics Charlotte's own sense of status incongruence. In her first position as a governess Charlotte was shocked to be reprimanded for appearing depressed, and resolved in future 'to command my feelings and to take what came' (*L.* i. 194). William also vows to function simply as an economic unit in a world where other people appear as potential enemies. His main weapon, like Charlotte's, is self-control – a rigid refusal to give others an advantage by allowing them access to his feelings, 'secure against... scrutiny as if I had had on a casque with the visor down' (*P.* 17).

Refusing aristocratic patronage, William submits to tedious labour as a clerk in his elder brother's northern factory, but although he presents 'a buckler of impenetrable indifference' (*P.* 20) to his brother's neglect, and would have 'endured in silence the rust and cramp of my best faculties', he feels 'like a plant growing in humid darkness out of the slimy walls of a well' (*P.* 25). Prompted by his friend Hunsden to take a risk with his future, he embarks for Belgium, where he finds work as a teacher, first in a boys' school and then also in the neighbouring girls' seminary. Here his self-control takes a form which we might not expect in a decorous Victorian novel; he needs it to resist the physical attractions of his pupils.

When he sees the girls, with their 'good features, ruddy, blooming complexions, large and brilliant eyes, forms full even to solidity.... I did not bear the first view like a stoic, I was dazzled' (*P.* 70). Soon, however, he is disillusioned:

> They were each and all supposed to have been reared in utter unconsciousness of vice – the precautions used to keep them ignorant, if not innocent, were innumerable; how was it then that scarcely one of those girls having attained the age of fourteen could look a man in the face with modesty and propriety? An air of bold, impudent flirtation or a loose, silly leer was sure to answer the most ordinary glance from a masculine eye. (*P.* 82)

A similar process ensues with the young Directress of the school, Mlle Reuter. William is encouraged to discuss her physical charms in conversation with M. Pelet, the headmaster of the adjacent boys' school (*P.* 80), although Pelet is engaged to marry Mlle Reuter himself, and the two of them are 'playing' William for amusement. Even indignation at discovering this trick, however, does not prevent William feeling that in dealing with Mlle Reuter, 'temptation penetrated to my senses' (P. 130). Despite Mlle Reuter's successful management of her school, both she and the schoolgirls are shown occupying traditional female positions, using their physical attractions to make an advantageous marriage. After her marriage, however, William discovers that Mme Pelet 'was herself caught in the meshes of the very passion with which she wished to entangle me' (P. 153).

As for Pelet, his 'bachelor's life had been passed in proper French style with due disregard to moral restraint – and I thought his married life promised to be very French also. He often boasted to me what a terror he had been to certain husbands of his acquaintance, I perceived it would not now be difficult to pay him back in his own coin' (P. 156). This is shocking content for a novel of the 1840s, and perhaps explains why *The Professor* was not published in Charlotte's lifetime. The sexual freedom of Byron and silver-fork romances is here expressed in the plain language of realism, as Crimsworth confesses: 'I was no pope – I could not boast infallibility – in short – if I stayed, the probability was that in three months' time, a practical Modern French novel would be in full process of concoction under the roof of the unsuspecting Pelet'. In rejecting this prospect, Crimsworth draws resolution from 'an example of...domestic treachery' which seems a veiled reference to Branwell. 'No golden halo of fiction was about this example', William writes, 'I saw it bare and real and it was very loathsome' (P. 157).

In the novel, however, sexual laxity is ascribed to the Belgians, whose Catholic education leaves them satisfied with lip-service to rules of obedience where Protestants would exercise self-discipline. The novel's antidote to Mlle Reuter is, therefore, a young Protestant woman named Frances Henri, half English, half Swiss, who supports herself by her own labour. Like Charlotte, Frances is small and slight, and her inner strength and intellect attract William in a different way from the Belgian women: 'I loved her, as she stood there, pennyless and parentless, for a sensualist – charmless, for me a treasure, my best object of sympathy on earth, thinking such thoughts as I thought, feeling such feelings as I felt...personification of discretion and forethought, of diligence and perseverance, of self-denial and self-control' (*P.* 141). The passage continues in this strain, embarrassing if you read it as Charlotte's self-portrait. When Frances and William lose sight of one another, however, Charlotte's new restraint keeps Frances's despair off-stage, her 'secret, inward wound' revealed only through a poem which William reads after their reunion (*P.* 185).

It is now, however, that Charlotte makes the theme of self-help her own, combining the fairy-tale younger brother motif with the 'kept-down' energy of the governess. William's love for Frances breeds 'a strong desire to do more, earn more, be more, possess more' in order to offer her a home (*P.* 146) and there follow some chapters of genuine economic struggle. Resigning his post at M. Pelet's, 'I forgot fastidiousness, conquered reserve, thrust pride from me: I asked, I persevered, I remonstrated, I dunned', and eventually he is successful (*P.* 177). In the usual pattern of the Bildungsroman, his economic success would be rewarded by marriage, which would cement his adult status in the community, and his story might properly end here. Instead, Charlotte offers us an early example of 'writing beyond the ending'.[20] Frances insists that after marriage she should aim to have her own school, as successful as her husband's. 'I like a contemplative life', she argues, 'but I like an active life better; I must act in some way and act with you.... people who are only in each other's company for amusement, never really like each other so well, or esteem each other so highly, as those who work together, and perhaps suffer together' (*P.* 189).

Beyond the normal ending, these last chapters of *The Professor* show us glimpses of a surprising married life. After the working day, William and Frances enjoy evenings of conversation in which Frances 'would vex, tease, pique me... with a wild and witty wickedness that made a perfect white demon of her while it lasted' (*P.* 211). The arrival of a son seems no obstacle to her management of her school, and the couple are so successful that they retire at the ages of 29 and 37, a rags-to-riches ascent equally accordant with a capitalist and a fairy-tale economy. Returning to England, they purchase a small estate. Here there is another surprise as the focus shifts to the education of their son – how best to fit him for the real world. At present, Victor's volatile spirits can be 'subjugated' by his mother's reason and love, but, William asks, 'will reason or love be the weapons with which in future the world will meet his violence? Oh no! . . . the lad will some day get blows instead of blandishments – kicks instead of kisses' (*P.* 222). Victor, therefore, must go to Eton, 'where, I suspect, his first year or two will be utter wretchedness', but where the suffering 'will ground him radically in the art of self-control' (*P.* 221–2).

Self-control, then, is the governing theme of the novel. Victor must be disciplined in order to become, like his parents, a self-reliant unit in the new economic climate. The question must have been vivid for Charlotte and Anne, as they worked on *The Professor* and *Agnes Grey* with the spectacle of Branwell's disgrace before them. Branwell, 'turned loose on the world' after a lenient home education, had failed in one situation after another, and both novels argue that while girls need more scope for independence, boys need more defence against temptation (*L.* i. 448).[21] In *The Professor*, self-control allows William to escape economic degradation and sexual disgrace, whereas the conventional surveillance of young women (like the Belgians in this book) leaves them free to engage in flirtation or seduction. Frances Henri, as William's female equivalent, offers a model of marriage in which active and intellectual companionship takes the place of sensuality. The price paid for self-control is high, however, and the novel's relentless emphasis on repression implies not an endorsement but a critique of the society that demands it.[22] William's world is one in which even children must be schooled to confront hostility, and where even companions in marriage, in the supposed calm of retirement, cannot entirely shed the watchful mask with which each faces the future.

3

Jane Eyre

'I care for myself. The more solitary, the more friendless,
the more unsustained I am, the more I will respect myself.' *(JE* 317)

Charlotte Brontë's *Jane Eyre* (1847) is now famous throughout
the world. It was an immediate success, going through edition
after edition. Her publisher's reader sat up half the night, her
publisher himself cancelled his engagements and the novelist
W. M. Thackeray lost a day's work to read it. Americans were
afflicted by 'a distressing mental epidemic, passing under the
name of the "Jane Eyre fever"'.[1] Queen Victoria called it 'really a
wonderful book'[2] and Emily Dickinson found it 'electric'. After a
hundred and sixty years it is still among the favourite books of
readers all over the world as well as being an object of academic
study; it has been translated into dozens of languages, adapted
many times in all media and imitated by numerous later
novelists.[3] Yet *The Professor*, written immediately before *Jane
Eyre*, was rejected nine times and has never been popular. How
do we account for *Jane Eyre's* extraordinary success?

'I have now written a great many books', Charlotte Brontë
wrote in 1839, but she was referring to her tales of imaginary
Angria. *The Professor* was the first work which she wrote with the
deliberate intention of engaging with the real world, and she
approached it with trepidation. It was, she wrote, like entering
'a distant country where every face was unknown & the
character of all the population an enigma' (A. 314). The hero
of *The Professor* is thus wary and watchful; his is an embattled
stance against the world and he seldom invites even the reader
to share his unguarded emotions. For William Crimsworth, self-
control amounts to a defensive armour.

Charlotte believed that by writing in this way she was
entering the world on its own terms, so her keen sense of irony

was aroused when she discovered that her book was being rejected because 'Publishers, in general...would have liked something more imaginative and poetical – something more consonant with a highly wrought fancy, with a native taste for pathos – with sentiments more tender – elevated – unworldly' (*P.* 3). Her wry reaction was turned into positive energy when, in 1847, the firm of Smith, Elder & Co. refused *The Professor,* but with the hint that 'a work in three volumes would meet with careful attention' (B. 621). Charlotte had, in fact, almost finished *Jane Eyre* while *The Professor* was going the rounds, and her correspondence with the earlier publishers seems to have encouraged a crucial change of approach: a more relaxed and trusting relationship with her readers.

In *Jane Eyre,* for the first time, Charlotte writes confidently as a woman, though still hiding her own identity under the title *Jane Eyre: An Autobiography: Edited by Currer Bell.* Although characters similar to Jane Eyre had appeared in 'Henry Hastings' and 'Caroline Vernon', their stories are narrated by a dashing male persona,[4] and although William Crimsworth in *The Professor* speaks from a quasi-feminine position, like that of 'some desolate tutor or governess' (*P.* 20), he is apologetic for his story, calling it 'not exciting', a tale which will interest only 'some individuals' who have 'toiled in the same vocation as myself' (*P.* 12). *The Professor,* moreover, has little sense of an audience; begun as a letter to a friend who never replies, it retains the quality of a 'dead letter', sent to an unknown and unresponsive recipient.

In *Jane Eyre,* by contrast, Charlotte seems to have taken courage to speak to, and even for, each 'desolate tutor and governess'. When Jane Eyre, sounding Charlotte's old theme, bewails the 'viewless fetters of an uniform and too still existence' (*JE* 116), she invokes a multitude of sympathisers:

> It is in vain to say human beings ought to be satisfied with tranquillity: they must have action; and they will make it if they cannot find it. Millions are condemned to a stiller doom than mine, and millions are in silent revolt against their lot. Nobody knows how many rebellions beside political rebellions ferment in the masses of life which people earth. Women are supposed to be very calm generally: but women feel just as men feel; they need exercise for their faculties, and a field for their efforts as much as their brothers

do; they suffer from too rigid a restraint, too absolute a stagnation, precisely as men would suffer; and it is narrow-minded in their more privileged fellow-creatures to say that they ought to confine themselves to making puddings and knitting stockings, to playing on the piano and embroidering bags. *(JE* 109)

The passage has been called a feminist manifesto, and it was undoubtedly the novel's passionate tone of protest which excited readers then as now; in the context of Victorian womanhood it was perceived as little short of revolutionary.[5] This polemical style is, however, not characteristic of the novel. From the beginning, Jane's story grips our attention not through persuasive speeches but through an invitation to share her experience.

Every reader was once a child, and so everyone has a vivid personal memory of the thwarted wrath with which each of us sometimes faced an unintelligible world. It is this fund of remembered passion which Charlotte Brontë invokes in her opening chapters, where ten-year-old Jane is assaulted and insulted by her insufferable cousin, John Reed, and, though 'habitually obedient' *(JE* 10), fights back 'like a mad cat' *(JE* 12). Although Jane 'was bewildered by the terror he inspired; because I had no appeal whatever against either his menaces or his inflictions' *(JE* 10), she still articulates her sense of undeserved suffering: '"Wicked and cruel boy!" I said. "You are like a murderer – you are like a slave-driver – you are like the Roman emperors!"' *(JE* 11). When her aunt in turn punishes her 'insurrection', her 'reason' cries out '"Unjust! – unjust!"' *(JE* 15).

The metaphor of slavery continues, but even while 'the mood of the revolted slave was still bracing me with its bitter vigour' *(JE* 14), the narrative shows a subtle shift of perspective. As Jane compares John with the Roman emperors, the narrative voice continues, 'I really saw in him a tyrant: a murderer' *(JE* 11), and this comment comes not from the immediate moment, but from a calmer vantage point. When Jane is locked up in the Red Room, this calmer voice continues: 'I could not answer the ceaseless inward question – *why* I thus suffered: now, at the distance of – I will not say how many years, I see it clearly. I was a discord in Gateshead Hall: I was like nobody there' *(JE* 15). Throughout the novel, the impact of immediate passion is juxtaposed with this calmer, older voice, which neither belittles the force of feeling nor demands the kind of repression which *The Professor* assumed as essential, but is the voice of humane reason. In one incident after another, the doubled voices of immediate Passion and reflective Reason address the question of endurance and revolt: when should one submit to authority, and when is rebellion justified?

This debate is not, however, conducted in abstract terms. The concrete environment of these opening scenes not only tells us about Jane's social situation, as a poor relation among unsympathetic relatives in a grand house, but also begins a metaphorical pattern which resonates with implications – as Terry Eagleton puts it, 'condensing into complex unity an accumulated host of subsidiary conflicts'.[6] We first see Jane seated in a window seat, 'shrined in double retirement. Folds of scarlet drapery shut in my view to the right hand; to the left were the clear panes of glass, protecting, but not separating me from the drear November day' (*JE* 8). Her position between inside and outside, between the threat of social abuse and the threat of elemental exposure, forms a visual correlative for what critics have called the liminal or threshold position of characters like Jane (or like the Brontës themselves) who are situated at 'a painfully ambiguous point in the social structure'.[7] As she sits in the window seat, the 'pale blank of mist and cloud' outside the window is echoed by the book she is reading, which describes 'the vast sweep of the Arctic Zone, and . . . the multiplied rigours of extreme cold' (*JE* 8), but this time it is the punitive social world which destroys her precarious safety as she is dragged through the scarlet curtains. In Mr Rochester's Thornfield Hall she will find an interior whose white and red colouring suggests a 'general blending of snow and fire' (*JE* 104), but this apparent balance is in turn destroyed when her blooming hopes are blighted by a metaphorical frost, becoming 'waste, wild, and white as pine-forests in wintry Norway' (*JE* 295). As she flees from the danger of becoming Rochester's mistress, the metaphors of exposure become reality, and outside the window of Moor House, wet, cold, hungry and exhausted, she looks in at a social group she longs to join. These shifting images of scenes inside and outside houses join a pattern of contrast between the cold and white of emotional deprivation and the fiery red of indignation and desire.

Jane's liminal position, like that of William Crimsworth in *The Professor*, results partly from her being an orphan, with no parents to define her position in society, and for a woman this entails both risk and opportunity. Florence Nightingale saw orphan status as essential for women in novels who would otherwise have no scope for action: 'the heroine has *generally* no family ties (almost *invariably* no mother), or, if she has, these do not interfere with her entire independence'.[8] A young woman securely placed within a family may have nothing to look forward to but 'the voyage in' to marriage and further domesticity, but the orphan child is to some extent released from such conformity, thrown on her own resources and not just allowed but forced to be self-reliant. When Mr Lloyd the apothecary suggests that Jane might go to school, she reflects that 'school would be a complete change: it implied a long journey... an entrance into a new life' (*JE* 25), and when she plans to leave Lowood, it takes 'courage to go forth' into the outside world (*JE* 85). The story of the orphan girl is thus able to mimic the male Bildungsroman, promising at last a 'voyage out'.[9]

Journeys, in fact, mark distinct stages of Jane's life. From Gateshead Hall and the Reed family, Jane travels to Mr Brocklehurst's Lowood School and then, in the longest section of the story, to Thornfield Hall, the seat of Mr Rochester. From here she runs away to Moor House where her Rivers cousins live, returning in the final section to find Rochester living at Ferndean. 'A new chapter in a novel is something like a new scene in a play', Jane writes (*JE* 93), and the five locations of *Jane Eyre* suggest a five-act drama, with exposition (Gateshead), development (Lowood), climax (Thornfield), reversal (Moor House) and resolution (Ferndean). There is even an alternation between scenes of passion (Gateshead and Thornfield) and those of reason or repression (Lowood and Moor House), with Ferndean as a balanced resolution. Because Jane takes journeys between these locations, her life story as a whole can be read as a journey towards self-knowledge or self-possession. These outlines, however, though useful, are reductive; 'the individual's journey to self-knowledge' is a form of words which suggests a universal template, discounting the specificities of Jane's experience as a nineteenth-century Englishwoman.

Jane's childhood rebellion frightens her aunt into sending

her away to Lowood, a charitable institution for the education of girls run by Mr Brocklehurst. The Lowood chapters, which draw on Charlotte Brontë's own memories of the Clergy Daughters' School at Cowan Bridge, are now remembered for the physical hardships they describe – cold and semi-starvation – and the gratuitous spite of the teacher Miss Scatcherd. More important, however, is the fact that Mr Brocklehurst, like his historical model, Carus Wilson, represents a powerful movement in nineteenth-century religious life. Working from the idea of original sin – that each child is born inheriting the fault of the first man, Adam – extreme evangelicals such as Carus Wilson believed that education meant suppression of natural, or 'animal' propensities.[10] Charlotte Brontë represents this real threat in a comically exaggerated form when Mr Brocklehurst insists that even naturally curly hair must be suppressed, since 'we are not to conform to nature: I wish these girls to be the children of Grace' (*JE* 64).

Jane Eyre fiercely resents and resists this dogma, arguing that if Miss Scatcherd tried to discipline her as she did Helen, 'I should get [the rod] from her hand; I should break it under her nose' (*JE* 55), but even before leaving Gateshead she begins to realize that the mood of insurrection would not sustain her. Furious with Mrs Reed for prejudicing Mr Brocklehurst against her, she repudiates her connection with this aunt-through-marriage: 'I am glad you are no relation of mine... and if any one asks me how I liked you, and how you treated me, I will say the very thought of you makes me sick, and that you treated me with miserable cruelty' (*JE* 36). Left 'winner of the field', she nevertheless soon realises that

> a child cannot quarrel with its elders... without experiencing afterwards the pang of remorse and the chill of reaction. A ridge of lighted heath, alive, glancing, devouring, would have been a meet emblem of my mind when I accused and menaced Mrs. Reed: the same ridge, black and blasted after the flames are dead, would have represented as meetly my subsequent condition, when half an hour's silence and reflection had shown me the madness of my conduct, and the dreariness of my hated and hating position (*JE* 37–8)

Jane's fury here is fuelled by neglect as well as injustice, and years later she will say to Aunt Reed that 'I am passionate, but not vindictive. Many a time, as a little child, I should have been glad to love you if you would have let me' (*JE* 240).

At Lowood, accordingly, Jane's fiery temper is tamed not by Mr Brocklehurst's repression, but by friendship and love. Even the gentle Christianity of Helen Burns, however, cannot persuade Jane that it is right to submit to unjust punishment, and she rejects the very word which is the keynote of *The Professor*: endurance. 'I could not comprehend this doctrine of endurance', cries the young Jane (*JE* 56). 'When we are struck at without a reason, we should strike back again very hard; I am sure we should – so hard as to teach the person who struck us never to do it again' (*JE* 57). It is important that Miss Temple, who becomes Jane's mentor and friend after Helen's death, gains her respect by listening to her tale of injustice and investigating its truth. Finding that Jane's version of events at Gateshead is true, she exonerates her before the whole school (*JE* 74). Miss Temple's forensic approach to injustice is an alternative to revolt, and the whole novel is informed by the language of the courtroom.[11] Nevertheless although Jane appeared, under Miss Temple's influence, to have 'given in allegiance to duty and order', the motive for her 'subdued' behaviour is lost when Miss Temple herself leaves: 'I tired of the routine of eight years in one afternoon. I desired liberty; for liberty I gasped'. The prayer is not heard: '"Then", I cried, half desperate, "Grant me at least a new servitude"' (*JE* 84–5).

Jane's position as governess at Thornfield Hall is not hard labour, but her life with the placid Mrs Fairfax and the tractable Adèle does indeed seem to her like 'servitude' because she feels imprisoned. At Lowood, she had 'longed to surmount' the hills which seemed to enclose 'prison-ground' (*JE* 85); now, at Thornfield, she finds the same physical boundary: 'I longed for a power of vision which might overpass that limit; which might reach the busy world, towns, regions full of life I had heard of but never seen' (*JE* 109). Her 'sole relief', walking in the third story corridor, was 'to open my inward ear to a tale that was never ended – a tale my imagination created, and narrated continuously; quickened with all of incident, life, fire, feeling, that I desired and had not in my actual existence' (*JE* 109).

When Jane meets Mr Rochester, later in this same chapter, the meeting appears like something from her imagination. We know that Jane as a child was familiar with tales of the supernatural – the ghost she fears in the Red Room, or the 'old fairy tales and older ballads' which Bessie tells in the nursery (*JE* 9). At 18, her mind is still full of 'all sorts of fancies bright and dark', intensified with a 'vigour and vividness beyond what childhood could give'. Thus, when she hears a horse's hooves on a lonely lane at dusk, she thinks of the 'North-of-England spirit, called a "Gytrash", which, in the form of horse, mule, or large dog, haunted solitary ways' (*JE* 112). Back at Thornfield Hall, Rochester reveals a similar frame of mind; when he saw her in the lane, he says, 'I thought unaccountably of fairy tales, and had half a mind to demand whether you had bewitched my horse' (*JE* 122). Neither of them seriously believes in fairies but, like Jane's peculiar pictures which are also shown on this occasion, the supernatural imagery opens up a playful imaginative world beyond mundane realism, an unexpected mental meeting-place for two strangers.

This first interview is the more remarkable when you realize that apart from Mr Lloyd and Mr Brocklehurst, Mr Rochester is the first adult man that Jane has encountered; he says she has 'the look of another world' (*JE* 121), but for men and women to encounter one another as aliens was not unusual in Victorian society, where middle- and upper-class boys would be sent away to school at puberty, and girls would meet them thereafter in severely constrained circumstances: a girl could marry a man whom she had never met alone. The second interview between Jane and Rochester is interesting, therefore, in that they use it to negotiate the terms on which they might meet; Jane agrees to accept Rochester's authority precisely because he seems willing to forget its more obvious source – that she is his 'paid subordinate' (*JE* 134). Their conversations are important in the novel, as Rochester's experience gives Jane vicarious access to the 'life, fire, feeling' which she craves. When Charlotte Brontë was 18, she wrote that London 'is to me [almost] as apocryphal as Babylon, or Nineveh, or ancient Rome' (*L.* i. 128), and Jane similarly writes, 'I had a keen delight in receiving the new ideas he offered, in imaging the new pictures he portrayed, and following him in thought through the new regions he disclosed'. Their conversations, in other words, combine the expansive excitement of Jane's imaginary visions with the comfort and reciprocity of friendship, so that she 'felt at times, as if he were my relation, rather than my master' (*JE* 146).

There are no verbatim accounts of the conversations at this time of consolidation in their relationship, but we must assume that the teasing, sparring quality which characterizes both their first and last dialogues must also have enlivened the intermediate time. Jane's exhilaration, however, in her sense of power over Rochester, her ability to keep him, as she says before their wedding, 'excellently entertained' with her 'needle of repartee' (*JE* 274, 273) is undercut by a sense of risk – a sense that the 'friendly frankness' (*JE* 146) which marks some parts of their interaction may give way at any time to a chasm of incomprehension when the conversation gets 'out of my depth' (*JE* 137), hinting at unfathomed secrets in Rochester's consciousness, or when he simply removes himself, without explanation, from her presence and her confidence.

A harrowing insecurity thus lies under their growing intimacy, 'where billows of trouble rolled under surges of joy' (*JE* 151), and the narrative of Jane's inner life is punctuated by Gothic interruptions signalling a mystery from which she is excluded. The chapter where she first meets Rochester begins with her sense of imprisonment, and her meditation on the 'millions' who suffer 'a stiller doom than mine', but immediately after this expansive 'feminist manifesto', she is recalled suddenly to her particular situation as her reverie is broken by a sinister laugh (*JE* 109–10). Virginia Woolf, writing about *Jane Eyre* in the 1920s, is critical of the 'awkward break' between Jane's polemical appeal against women's lot and what seems like an abrupt return to the plot.[12] Later feminists, however, have seen the conjunction as anything but accidental, as the novel later reveals that the laugh, unintelligible at the time, is that of the mad Mrs Rochester, ironically confined close by where Jane paces the third story corridor like a caged animal (*JE* 109), and the parallel images of confinement form another pattern in the novel:

> Here at the center of a novel about one woman's struggle for independence and love is a woman who is utterly restrained and considered socially dead, who, nevertheless, breaks through her restraints and occasionally wreaks havoc in the house of which she is the hidden, titular mistress. ...Woman under too rigid a restraint – a woman offered as an object in a marriage settlement – displays in perverse ways the power that she is continually denied.[13]

This is Nancy Pell, writing in 1977, but two years later this idea of the parallel between Jane and Bertha was given enduring expression by Sandra Gilbert and Susan Gubar in *The Madwoman in the Attic: The Woman Writer and the Nineteenth-Century Literary Imagination*.[14]

One result of living under restraint or surveillance is that the victim (as we see in *The Professor*) develops a social mask as a defence against intrusion. When Robert Southey deplored the young Charlotte Brontë's flights of fancy, she replied that 'I carefully avoid any appearance of pre-occupation and eccentricity, which might lead those I live amongst to suspect the nature of my pursuits' (*L. i.* 169), and in *Jane Eyre* a servant at Gateshead declares that despite Jane's passionate outbursts, 'she's an underhand little thing: I never saw a girl of her age with so much cover' (*JE* 12). Gilbert and Gubar argue that just as women in the nineteenth century learned to survive in society by repressing unacceptable rage, so women writers at this time preserve a surface of propriety, 'projecting their rebellious impulses not into their heroines but into mad or monstrous women'. They see *Jane Eyre* as the paradigmatic text for this process, by which 'female authors dramatize their own self-division, their desire both to accept the strictures of patriarchal society and to reject them'.[15]

Nineteenth-century readers saw the mad Mrs Rochester either as a sensational means of adding excitement to the story, or as a mechanical plot device, creating suspense by keeping Jane and Rochester apart. In the twentieth century, Freudian theories led readers to see her as a warning against a sexual excess which Jane must renounce to achieve social acceptability. Gilbert and Gubar, by contrast, present Jane's psychological repression as equivalent to Bertha's physical imprisonment, and their analysis is valuable in recognizing the force of structural patterning in the novel. It does not, however, sufficiently acknowledge the persistence, and expression, of Jane's own rebellious spirit. Aunt Reed is taken aback by the fact that for nine years Jane 'could be patient and quiescent under any treatment, and in the tenth break out all fire and violence' (*JE* 239–40), and this is a pattern which is repeated throughout her story.

The madwoman in the attic is not entirely a figment of Charlotte's imagination. There are several examples which would have been known to her of insane people incarcerated and kept more or less secret.[16] This particular madwoman is, however, presented through the medium of Gothic sensation – the eerie laugh, the setting fire to Rochester's bed, the tearing of Jane's wedding veil – which gives the novel an uncanny dimension. This description is not to dismiss these devices as 'mere' sensation. As Freud explained, an uncanny effect is produced not by completely alien manifestations but by something familiar which we have made an effort to forget – 'something which ought to have remained hidden but has come to light', something which in shorthand is called 'the return of the repressed'.[17] Jane's anger, repressed by social conformity, might well, therefore, appear uncanny when its outbursts are mirrored by Bertha's inarticulate violence, and it is important that just as Freud encouraged his patients to achieve the 'talking cure', so Jane is repeatedly saved by defining her outrage.

Rochester values Jane's calm self-possession as she receives his cryptic hints about his former life, but he also wishes to breach this self-control and provoke her into acknowledging her love for him. His impersonation of the gypsy woman simply confirms that in Jane's character, 'Reason sits firm and holds the reins, and she will not let the feelings burst away and hurry her to wild chasms. The passions may rage furiously, like true heathens, as they are; and the desires may imagine all sorts of vain things: but judgment shall still have the last word in every argument' (JE 201). At last, however, he presses his pretence of engagement to Blanche Ingram to the point of cruelty; when he proposes with apparent equanimity that Jane depart to Bitternutt Lodge, she once more 'break[s] out all fire and violence': 'the vehemence of emotion, stirred by grief and love within me, was claiming mastery, and struggling for full sway; and asserting a right to predominate: to overcome, to live, rise, and reign at last; yes, – and to speak' (JE 252). Her tone, in this declaration of love, is one of indignation, suggesting that although she does not understand Rochester's plan she nevertheless feels that his control of the situation is, once again, 'unjust':

> Do you think I am an automaton? – a machine without feelings? and can bear to have my morsel of bread snatched from my lips, and my drop of living water dashed from my cup? Do you think, because I

am poor, obscure, plain, and little, I am soulless and heartless? – You think wrong! – I have as much soul as you, – and full as much heart! And if God had gifted me with some beauty, and much wealth, I should have made it as hard for you to leave me, as it is now for me to leave you. I am not talking to you now through the medium of custom, conventionalities, nor even of mortal flesh: – it is my spirit that addresses your spirit; just as if both had passed through the grave, and we stood at God's feet, equal – as we are! (*JE* 253)

'As we are!' echoes Rochester to this speech of Jane's, but during the period of their engagement it appears that although he applauds Jane's casting aside of class barriers, he still expects the privileges of his sex. The images of slavery reappear, though in a softened and ironic frame, as Jane compares Rochester's possessive smile with one that 'a sultan might, in a blissful and fond moment, bestow on a slave his gold and gems had enriched' (*JE* 269). This re-emergence of slavery in the text is, for the modern reader, the 'return of the repressed' of a whole culture rather than an individual, since it reminds us now of what has been invisible to a century of readers: the fact that Rochester's wealth derives from slave plantations in the West Indies. In the late twentieth century, in fact, the dismantling of the British Empire has given rise to the critical stance called postcolonialism, and just as feminism was responsible for re-reading classic texts in the context of the contemporary position of women, so postcolonial criticism opens a hitherto invisible perspective on novels like *Jane Eyre* by revealing the extent to which its characters depend on colonial wealth.

Well before *The Madwoman in the Attic,* the novelist Jean Rhys had imagined a West Indian biography for Bertha Mason in her haunting novel, *Wide Sargasso Sea* (1966), which presents Bertha (under her original name, Antoinette) as the heiress of plantation riches and thus as a victim of the male relatives who treat her as a medium of exchange – her wealth for Rochester's English lineage. Several subsequent critics have gone further than this, trying to read Bertha – whose mother was a 'Creole' – as representing an enslaved race (*JE* 290).[18] The postcolonial critic Gayatri Spivak, however, writes pointedly that in both *Jane Eyre* and *Wide Sargasso Sea* it is not Bertha who is the invisible victim of colonialism, but the black slaves who produced their wealth.[19]

The slave metaphors which Jane invokes during her engagement to Rochester are rather different, deriving not from plantation life but from oriental sexual slavery. Charlotte Brontë would have known the famous portrait of Byron in oriental dress, and had read his 'Turkish Tales' in which the heroes rescue harem inmates from self-indulgent and autocratic Pashas. In Charlotte's Angrian tales her hero, the Duke of Zamorna, is referred to as 'Sultan' because of his domination of women, and in *Jane Eyre* Rochester echoes Jane's image when he states that he 'would not exchange this one little English girl for the grand Turk's whole seraglio'. Whereas in Angria, however, the stories of Zamorna's intrigues are told by a witty male narrator, in *Jane Eyre* Jane herself takes control of the narrative:

> 'I'll not stand you an inch in the stead of a seraglio,' I said; 'so don't consider me an equivalent for one: if you have a fancy for anything in that line, away with you, sir, to the bazaars of Stamboul without delay; and lay out in extensive slave-purchases some of that spare cash you seem at a loss to spend satisfactorily here.'
>
> 'And what will you do, Janet', while I am bargaining for so many tons of flesh and such an assortment of black eyes?'
>
> 'I'll be preparing myself to go out as a missionary to preach liberty to them that are enslaved – your Harem inmates amongst the rest. I'll get admitted there, and I'll stir up mutiny; and you, three-tailed bashaw as you are, sir, shall in a trice find yourself fettered amongst our hands: nor will I, for one, consent to cut your bonds till you have signed a charter, the most liberal that despot ever yet conferred.' (*JE* 269)

It is a remarkable passage, but one open to different readings; on the one hand, it appears to situate Jane as a champion and 'sister' to the oppressed women of other races. On the other hand, as Susan Meyer argues, 'the use of the racial "other" as a metaphor for class and gender struggles in England commodifies colonial subjects as they exist in historical actuality and transforms them into East or West "Indian ink", ink with which to write a novel about ending oppression in England'.[20] Spivak's position is equally critical, as she attacks western feminists for focussing on Jane's own struggle to achieve personhood, seeing nothing in the novel but 'the psychobiography of the militant female subject'.[21] We have to admit that Charlotte Brontë, though progressive

42

in many respects, was a woman of her time in terms of colonial possessions. Although present-day readers may become aware of the hidden injustices of imperialism which underpin this novel, there is no doubt that the project of *Jane Eyre* itself is indeed to guide Jane to full self-possession, and that Bertha is important in the pattern of contrasts and parallels which define the novel's heroine. After the failed wedding, Rochester forces those present to confront the contrast between '*my wife*', now revealed as a figure hardly human, which 'snatched and growled like some strange wild animal', and 'this young girl, who stands so grave and quiet at the mouth of hell' (*JE* 293–4).

Jane's self-control has been tested during the period of engagement. Spurred by Mrs Fairfax's comment, that 'gentlemen in [Mr Rochester's] station are not accustomed to *marry* their governesses' (*JE* 265; my emphasis), Jane has used her wit and her tongue to keep him at bay, and although she talks of avoiding 'a bathos of sentiment' (*JE* 273), the real danger is sexual surrender. Her self-confidence in keeping him 'rather cross and crusty' (*JE* 274) is built on their earlier conversations, but also draws on the fairy-tale model of Bluebeard. Significantly, the first time that Jane hears Bertha's laugh, she has just noticed that the 'two rows of small black doors' in the third story corridor remind her of 'Bluebeard's castle' (*JE* 107), and now she acts the part of Scheherezade, delaying the moment, not of death, but of sexual capitulation, with the 'needle of repartee' (*JE* 273). Her anticipation of union is not, in fact, as blissful as one might expect: she writes, 'there was no putting off the day that advanced – the bridal day' (*JE* 275). Jane resents the dependent status of a married woman, rejecting Rochester's attempts to adorn her with gifts and writing to her uncle Eyre in an attempt to establish independent standing.

Despite the obvious contrast, moreover, between Jane's self-control and Bertha's wild abandon, the parallel between them is still strong. In the scene following their confrontation, where Rochester tempts Jane to stay with him as his mistress, he repudiates Bertha as 'intemperate and unchaste' (*JE* 306). Jane, however, is no stranger to desire. After Bertha set fire to Rochester's bed, Jane and Rochester were alone together in his bedroom and Rochester's lingering farewell, delivered with 'strange fire in his look', keeps Jane 'tossed on a buoyant but unquiet sea' (*JE* 151) all night. For a post-Freudian reader, the symbolism of the burning bed is almost too blatant, and in the interview after the failed wedding Jane feels Rochester's seduction as visceral: 'a hand of fiery iron grasped my vitals' (*JE* 315). Her emotion is so intense that she describes herself as 'insane – quite insane: with my veins running fire'. The imagery of fire runs between them: Rochester 'seemed to devour me with his flaming glance: physically, I felt, at the moment, powerless as stubble exposed to the draught and glow of a furnace'. The power of free decision conferred by Jane's orphan status itself now seems to work for surrender – 'my very Conscience and Reason turned traitors against me', she writes, crying 'Who in the world cares for *you*? or who will be injured by what you do?'.

Jane's answer to herself is one of the most famous, and most contentious, passages in the book: 'Still indomitable was the reply – "*I* care for myself. The more solitary, the more friendless, the more unsustained I am, the more I will respect myself.' Quoted thus, the statement can be read as an unequivocal declaration of independence. It continues, however:

> I will keep the laws given by God; sanctioned by man. I will hold to the principles received by me when I was sane, and not mad – as I am now. Laws and principles are not for the times when there is no temptation: they are for such moments as this, when body and soul rise in mutiny against their rigour.... If at my individual convenience I might break them, what would be their worth?... Preconceived opinions, foregone determinations, are all I have at this hour to stand by: there I plant my foot. (*JE* 317)

Modern feminists, believing in a woman's right to self-determination, are apt to be disappointed by Jane's position here, seeing it as a mere capitulation to convention. The speech raises in its most contentious form the question which has haunted the novel from the beginning: when is it right to submit to external authority, and when is it right to rebel?

In judging Jane's decision to leave Rochester at this point, we might remember that although Aunt Reed and Mr Brocklehurst represented authority in her youth, she rebelled against them because their power appeared to her unjust; her reason could not endorse it. The 'preconceived opinions, foregone determinations' which Jane now invokes, however, do not represent a merely external authority, but one which she herself has endorsed when she was 'sane'. Crucial among her 'preconceived opinions' is her response to Rochester's account of his earlier mistresses: 'Hiring a mistress is the next worse thing to buying a slave', he says, and his choice of words resonates with the novel's established system of references to slavery and revolt (*JE* 311). The 'insanity' of sexual surrender would lead to the 'slavery' of sexual subjection, and Jane cannot voluntarily enslave herself. She tells us that 'I felt the truth of these words; and I drew from them the certain inference, that if I were so far to forget myself... as... to become the successor of these poor girls, he would one day regard me with the same feeling which now in his mind desecrated their memory' (*JE* 312).

A Victorian readership would be much more aware than we now are of the social ignominy of the 'fallen woman'. In one of the many Victorian stage versions of *Jane Eyre*, a grown-up John Reed tricks Blanche Ingram into a false marriage – a clear parallel to Rochester's plan – and then abandons her, leaving her to lament the lot of the 'cast off mistress': 'a woman of the streets – the woman, who suffers all the degradation, losing position, friends, station, is an outcast whose momentary sin no repentance can palliate, no reparation condone – the man, the betrayer, whose base passion has ruined the heart he should have cherished, society receives with open arms – he is free to ruin other homes, and send more innocent souls to perdition'.[22]

In Charlotte Brontë's novel, it is ironic that in leaving Rochester to preserve her self-possession, Jane becomes to all appearances a fallen woman – destitute and literally prostrate on the ground – but the next section of the novel demands not only self-control but almost self-negation as she conceals her real identity. Her rescue by the Rivers family, who prove to be her cousins, is part of the rather schematic patterning of the novel, but the detail of her interaction with her cousin St John is chillingly persuasive. Here is another extreme evangelical, who cannot, however, be dismissed as a comic grotesque. His self-control, in denying himself the love of Rosamond Oliver, is an extreme exaggeration of what Jane has demanded of herself, but his 'voyage out' into the role of missionary is very different from the one she imagines for herself, liberating the inmates of the harem. We cannot doubt that St John's aim is to subject his converts to the same Calvinist repression that he exacts from himself, and that his presence in India would endorse the British Raj.

Jane's response to St John is paradigmatic of her behaviour throughout the novel: 'I know no medium: I never in my life have known any medium in my dealings with positive, hard characters, antagonistic to my own, between absolute submission and determined revolt. I have always faithfully observed the one, up to the very moment of bursting, sometimes with volcanic vehemence, into the other' (*JE* 400). In this case, she is on the point of irrevocable submission – agreeing to go with him to India, even while feeling that 'my iron shroud contracted round me' (*JE* 404), until he makes marriage a condition. Although , with her 'veins running fire', she had felt the threat of Rochester's attraction like a 'furnace' (*JE* 317), St John would require her 'to keep the fire of my nature continually low, to compel it to burn inwardly and never utter a cry, though the imprisoned flame consumed vital after vital' (*JE* 408). St John's incomprehension of her refusal reveals to Jane the effective tyranny of what he proposes: 'the veil fell from his hardness and despotism'. Tellingly, Jane says she 'took courage. I was with ... one whom, if I saw good, I might resist' (*JE* 406). Resist she does; when he insists that a kind of love would follow their marriage, she 'bursts' into 'revolt': '"I scorn your idea of love," I could not help saying, as I rose up and stood before him. . . . "I scorn the counterfeit sentiment you offer: yes, St John, and I scorn you when you offer it"' (*JE* 408).

In this context, the apparently supernatural call which Jane hears from Rochester appears, as she says, not 'witchcraft' but 'the work of nature' (*JE* 420). We can read it as the voice of Jane's own desire, and as she flees back to Rochester, the question must arise: would she have gone to live with him if Mrs Rochester had still been alive? The question hovers over the end of the novel, impossible to answer, since in its last sections the imagery of fire which has accompanied Jane's passions becomes a purgative reality, destroying Bertha and chastening Rochester's despotism. Some modern feminists are irritated by this ending, feeling that Jane's radical revolt has settled too easily into a happy-ever-after which needs no social reform, but only the right man. Charlotte Brontë has, however, manipulated her plot in order to give Jane the financial independence she needs in order to assert social, as well as spiritual, equality with Rochester, and in an early-Victorian context, Jane's rebellion against convention is not insignificant. Margaret Oliphant credited Charlotte Brontë with having created a new kind of relationship between men and women, in which their 'furious love-making' is 'but a wild declaration of the "Rights of Woman" in a new aspect'.[23]

The enduring appeal of *Jane Eyre* must, in fact, lie in its curious mixture of radical and conservative elements, which has made it both a template for Mills & Boon (or Harlequin) romances, and an inspiration to feminists. In historical reality, society did not offer much scope for self-fulfilment for women in Jane's situation, and her negotiation of a companionate marriage in which the partners accept one another as equals, in which they 'talk...all day long' (*JE* 451) and yet are drawn together by physical desire, is not a negligible achievement. The novel's mixed narrative mode, moreover, enhances the atmosphere of success by placing the novel's social realism within a fairy-tale structure of coincidence and bequest, while its metaphorical system, weaving a network of allusions to injustice, slavery, revolt, imprisonment and madness, resonates with larger implications. An oddity which has puzzled generations of readers is that the novel ends not with the heroine's marriage but with the near-death ecstasy of St John Rivers. This, of course, is the alternative life which Jane might have chosen, and while ostensibly praising this 'high master-spirit' Jane also reminds us that St John's creed is 'Whosoever will come after me, let him deny himself' (*JE* 452). Jane Eyre can be a heroine for the modern world because she does not deny herself in submission to a supernatural cause or a social convention, but only in defence of her self-respect. Questioning authority and speaking out against injustice, she forges the self-reliance from which reciprocity can grow.

4

Shirley

'Is this enough? Is it to live?' (*S*. 149)

The success of *Jane Eyre* opened a wider window on the world for Charlotte Brontë. Although she was able to shelter under her pseudonym for a year or more, correspondence with her publisher, George Smith, and even more importantly with his intelligent and sympathetic reader, William Smith Williams, brought her into immediate contact with the cultural life of London, introducing 'such light and life to the torpid retirement where we lie like dormice' (*L*. i. 580). Since Williams also sent current journals and parcels of new books, 'for the first time in their lives [Charlotte and her sisters] were able to see and read the newest books as they were published instead of having to wait for them to be available in the circulating and subscription libraries' (B. 649).

Jane Eyre was published in October 1847 and its reviews began to appear in 1848, the 'Year of Revolutions' in Europe and the year of the final flare-up of Chartism in England, and some readers saw a connection. By January 1848 a version of *Jane Eyre* was on stage at the Victoria Theatre (the 'Old Vic'), a notorious hotbed of Chartism,[1] and by December Elizabeth Rigby (later Lady Eastlake) declared 'that the tone of the mind and thought which has overthrown authority and violated every code human and divine abroad, and fostered Chartism and rebellion at home, is the same which has also written Jane Eyre'.[2]

There is irony in the fact that Charlotte, with her conservative opinions and adulation of the Duke of Wellington, should be seen as the champion of insurrection, especially as her views even of legitimate military glory were considerably muted since the days of Angria. Writing to Margaret Wooler in March 1848, she confesses that '"the pomp and circumstance of war" have quite lost in my eyes their factitious glitter', while as for 'convulsive revolutions', they 'put back the world in all that is good, check civilisation, bring the dregs of society to its surface'. She prays that 'England may be spared the spasms, cramps and frenzy-fits now contorting the Continent' (L. ii. 48), but the danger was not so distant. During the early months of 1848 thousands of unemployed and desperate textile workers gathered on the moors around Haworth and in the nearby towns of Keighley and Bradford, and as Juliet Barker notes, Charlotte 'could not have stepped out of the front door of her home without seeing the suffering all around her' (B. 655).

These circumstances were the more disturbing for Charlotte since her agreement with Smith, Elder & Co. gave them the right to her next two novels, and the current climate seemed to demand a topical subject. The genre of the 'social-problem' novel was already well-established with such novels as Fanny Trollope's *Michael Armstrong, Factory Boy* (1840) and Benjamin Disraeli's *Sybil* (1845) though Elizabeth Gaskell's *Mary Barton* (1848), which explores with passionate sympathy the plight of desperate Manchester textile workers, appeared only after Charlotte had begun work on her new novel.

Charlotte's consciousness of the expectation raised by the success of *Jane Eyre* was heightened by the sheer variety of its reviews; the experience of hearing her book discussed from so many viewpoints made her aware as never before that her audience included well-informed, confident, opinionated people. She also began to receive letters from other novelists, in particular W. M. Thackeray and George Henry Lewes, and she seemed alarmed when Williams compared her with such 'eminent writers', pointing out that 'Mr Thackeray, Mr Dickens, Mrs Marsh &c., doubtless enjoyed facilities for observation such as I have not; certainly they possess a knowledge of the world... such as I can lay no claim to' (L. i. 546). Charlotte thus professed herself reluctant to address current social issues directly. 'Situations which I do not understand, and cannot personally inspect', she wrote to Williams, 'I would not for the world meddle with, lest I should make even a more ridiculous mess of the matter than Mrs Trollope did in her "Factory Boy"' (L. ii. 23).

In the event, however, she only distanced the material by

setting her new novel in the past, in the years 1811–12, the period of the Luddite machine-breaking which offered clear parallels to the current Chartist unrest. Her self-deprecating expressions, moreover, are belied by the ambitious and panoramic scope of the book which she eventually called *Shirley*. The novel is framed by Wellington's Peninsular campaign – the war which was brought home to west Yorkshire when the British government's 'Orders in Council' cut off markets for Yorkshire wool, forcing manufacturers to lay off workers whose livelihood was already threatened by new labour-saving machinery, prompting the self-styled 'Luddites' to break the machines and even to destroy the mills.[3] Charlotte would have read Lord Byron's 1812 maiden speech to the House of Lords, where he describes with relentless irony how the workers, 'instead of rejoicing at these improvements in arts so beneficial to mankind, conceived themselves to be sacrificed to improvements in mechanism'.[4] Closer to home, Charlotte knew not only Patrick's stories of the attack on Rawfold's Mill (B. 52–3), but also those of Miss Wooler, whose Roe Head School was in the same district.

Compared with Gaskell and the other 'social problem' novelists, Charlotte's approach to her topic is curiously impersonal. Rather than focussing on the plight of the workers, she gives us a spread of middle-class opinion, from the high Tory Church-and-State clergyman, Mr Helstone, who will defend property and patriotic war at all costs, to the free-thinking republican Mr Yorke, who deplores the war with France and sympathizes with the workers. In the centre is the nearest the novel has to a hero, the exiled Belgian manufacturer Robert Gérard Moore, the master of Hollow's Mill, epitomizing the entrepreneurial ambition promoted by the industrial revolution. Motivated only by his need to renew production and succeed in a competitive market, he is opposed to the war but harshly unsympathetic to the workers. These positions are almost schematically displayed in Volume i, chapters 2–4, in which these unlikely allies gather at Hollow's Mill, awaiting the delivery of machinery which proves to have been waylaid and smashed before arrival. These scenes of dialogue between sharply differentiated characters are reminiscent of Charlotte aged 13 boasting of her comprehensive grasp of the political scene: 'we take the "Leeds Intelligencer", Tory, and the "Leeds Mercury", Whig....We see the "John Bull"; it is a high Tory, very violent' (G. 69). As for the workers, Charlotte's treatment is almost laconic. In Volume i, chapter 5, child workers arrive at Hollow's Mill: 'Let us hope they have enough to eat', the narrator comments, 'it would be a pity were it otherwise' (S. 53). With an implied sneer at Fanny Trollope's novel, she writes, 'child-torturers, slave masters and drivers, I consign to the hands of jailors; the novelist may be excused from sullying his page with the record of their deeds' (S. 52). Moore's later confrontations with the workers reveal their local spokesmen to be worthless men – the drunken Methodist Moses Barraclough (S. 114–16) and the 'half-crazed weaver' Michael Hartley (S. 532), while the more serious demagogues, as in Dickens's later 'industrial' novel, *Hard Times* (1854), are represented as 'strangers: emissaries from the large towns "down-draughts", bankrupts, men always in debt and often in drink – men who had nothing to lose, and much – in the way of character, cash, and cleanliness – to gain' (S. 322).

Only one worker, William Farren, is singled out to make a serious and moving representation of the workers' undeserved suffering, although, like Dickens's Stephen Blackpool, who famously analyses industrial relations as 'a muddle' (Book ii, chapter 5), Farren can only see that things are 'sorely acrooked' (S. 117). Like Stephen Blackpool, Farren is treated as a special case. Readers might be forgiven for imagining the Farrens' cottage as an isolated rural dwelling instead of one of hundreds necessary to run Moore's mill, and he receives charitable relief from the Revd Hall, from Mr Yorke and even from Robert Moore. Provided with alternative work as a gardener, he is removed from the scene of dissent.

Dickens, like Gaskell, advocates charitable intervention, plus a change of heart on the part of manufacturers, as the only discernible answer to working-class suffering, and later in Charlotte's novel, Shirley herself does organize large-scale charity with the express intent 'to *prevent* mischief' (S. 225). These good intentions are, however, undercut: Robert Moore is proved right when he says that 'eleemosynary relief never yet tranquillized the working-classes', who feel that 'they ought not to be in a position to need that humiliating relief' and, needing it, 'they hate us worse than ever' (*S.* 245). The workers still attack Hollow's Mill and Moore is still shot from behind a wall.

Juliet Barker finds it 'extraordinary that a writer with such a deserved reputation for realism, truth and feeling did not allow the contemporary sufferings of the Chartists to inform her portrayal of the Luddites' (B. 655). She sees it as 'ironic that despite Charlotte's abundant opportunities to observe the suffering of the poor during periods of distress, she relied instead on her reading, conscientiously consulting the files of the *Leeds Mercury*' for 1812–14 (B. 656). Heather Glen, however, recalling Charlotte's youthful familiarity with newspapers, argues that her response is 'rather more canny than this'. Instead of a simple need to clarify the facts, Glen argues that Charlotte's is 'a more sophisticated awareness that "facts" are refracted, always, through differing voices and perspectives; that information is a contested, opinion a constructed thing'.[5]

The disconcerting thing about *Shirley* is that its narrative voice offers no arbitrating analysis of these competing positions. *Shirley* is the first of Charlotte's fictions to be written in the third person, but instead of exchanging the immediacy of first-person intimacy for the authority of third-person omniscience, this narrator seems wary of assuming any settled relationship with the reader. The tone of the narrative varies widely from caustic humour through the bitter voice of experience to moving engagement with individuals, and its frame varies from true omniscience through teasing questions to the limited view of a character in a particular scene. Sometimes the narrator claims knowledge even of future events, outside the frame of the novel, as when the future death of Jessy Yorke (modelled on Martha Taylor) is introduced into a scene where she is a very lively child (*S.* 128). Towards the end of the novel, by contrast, the narrator seems to withdraw, leaving the important scenes of Robert Moore's proposal to Shirley, and Louis Moore's courtship, to a reported conversation and to extracts from Louis's journal.[6]

The shifting narrative viewpoint is matched by disconcerting changes in focus from public to private events and from one set of characters to another. G. H. Lewes perceptively comments that '*Shirley*... is not a picture; but a portfolio of random sketches for one or more pictures'.[7] Lewes undoubtedly meant this as a negative judgement, and Rebecca Fraser, writing in

1988, agrees: 'artistically, the novel is quite a failure, lacking the unity of *Jane Eyre*'.[8] For Heather Glen, however, this refusal to take a consistent position reflects 'the open-endedness of unknowing', offering 'a vision of the nature of the social world that is sharply, suggestively different from that of any other novel published in England in these years'.[9]

The novel opens with a refusal of melodrama which recalls the Preface to *The Professor*, but where that Preface adopts a tongue-in-cheek irony, the opening of *Shirley* is thoroughly worldly and sardonic, tantalizing the reader with the possibility of 'a taste of the exciting' later in the story, but offering immediately a dish of 'cold lentils and vinegar without oil' (*S. 5*). This first chapter concerns itself not with the defence of Hollow's Mill, but with a Rabelaisian scene of riot and gluttony involving three church curates – a scene which drew many objections (not least from Charlotte's own publishers) as not only in bad taste but as inessential to the novel's main subject. Gilbert and Gubar, however, are surely right when they point out that it opens a governing theme of hunger, whether physical or emotional.[10]

This theme gathers emotional power in Volume i, chapters 5 and 6, which introduce Caroline Helstone, the niece of the Revd Helstone and cousin of Robert Moore. Caroline, unlike Jane Eyre, is quietly beautiful and although spirited and independent in thought, is less volcanic in behaviour, even submitting to the exacting domestic instruction of Robert's sister, Hortense. In Volume i, chapter 6 we see her attempting, in a resourceful and clever way, to perform what was becoming known as 'woman's mission' – to exert a civilizing influence on men.[11] By reading Shakespeare's *Coriolanus* with Robert she hopes to make him realize how destructive – and self-destructive – is his proud and uncharitable attitude to his workers. Her efforts are hardly successful, but the scene is charming, and sends Caroline home 'excited and joyously troubled' (*S. 82*).

The next chapter (Volume i, chapter 7), however, finds the narrative voice in the mode of bitter experience. Caroline, reflecting on her evening with Robert, thinks innocently that 'when people love, the next step is they marry' (*S. 84*), and since she now feels sure that Robert loves her, and she certainly loves him, her future looks rosy. Where the older narrative voice of

Jane Eyre is gentle and explanatory in relation to the mistakes of youth, however, this voice is unrelenting. 'Caroline Helstone was just eighteen years old', we read, and 'at eighteen, the school of Experience is still to be entered, and her humbling, crushing, grinding, but yet purifying and invigorating lessons are yet to be learnt' (*S.* 82–3). The day after Caroline's happy evening with Robert, he fails to acknowledge that evening's 'nameless charm', and the narrator's comment is remorseless:

> You expected bread, and you have got a stone; break your teeth on it, and don't shriek because the nerves are martyrized: do not doubt that your mental stomach – if you have such a thing – is strong as an ostrich's – the stone will digest. You held out your hand for an egg, and fate put into it a scorpion. Show no consternation: close your fingers firmly upon the gift; let it sting through your palm. Never mind: in time, after your hand and arm have swelled and quivered long with torture, the squeezed scorpion will die, and you will have learned the great lesson how to endure without a sob. (*S.* 89–90)

Thus, the novel which begins with public affairs seems to broach a more conventional trajectory – a love story – only to cut it brutally off with a return to Charlotte's old theme of 'endurance'. Rebecca Fraser complains that the novel 'never quite makes up its mind whether it is primarily a novel of social protest or a straightforward love story',[12] but the connections are in fact inexorable: the country is locked in a foreign war which it cannot win but dare not abandon, so that manufacturers cannot sell their cloth but must still innovate for market advantage, putting marriage with a penniless girl out of the question. Instead of a 'straightforward love story', Charlotte Brontë now offers a relentless examination of the options facing a woman who does not marry. 'When a woman has a little family to rear and educate and a houshold [sic] to conduct, her hands are full, her vocation is evident', she had written to Williams in May 1848 (*L.* ii. 66), but for Caroline Helstone the problem of her life resolves itself into a question, 'How am I to get through this day?' (*S.* 92), or, more desperately, 'What am I to do to fill the interval of time which spreads between me and the grave?' (*S.* 149).[13]

Even during her happy evening with Robert, Caroline has expressed a wish for employment and imagines herself happy as a clerk in his counting-house – an ironic wish when we remember that William Crimsworth's spell as a factory clerk made him feel 'like a plant growing in humid darkness out of the slimy walls of a well' (*P.* 25). The only other employment she can imagine is to be a governess, but Shirley's ex-governess warns her away from the 'dreadful crushing of the animal spirits, the ever prevailing sense of friendlessness and homelessness' of a life which can be 'sedentary, solitary, constrained, joyless, toilsome' (*S.* 316). The fact that Mrs Pryor's warning incorporates extracts from Elizabeth Rigby's review of *Jane Eyre* shows how profoundly Charlotte had resented that account of the governess's life. In any case, although Caroline is effectively an orphan, her freedom of action is absolutely curtailed by her uncle and guardian, Mr Helstone, a masterly portrait of masculine power which combines apparent beneficence with effectual tyranny.

Helstone represents an extreme version of the current doctrine of 'separate spheres' for men and women. He has effectively killed his own wife through benign neglect:

> He thought, so long as a woman was silent, nothing ailed her, and she wanted nothing. If she did not complain of solitude, solitude, however continued, could not be irksome to her. If she did not talk and put herself forward, express a partiality for this, an aversion to that, she had no partialities or aversions, and it was useless to consult her tastes. (*S.* 45)

Caroline is now subjected to the same regime, and when she does venture to ask for employment, or change, is met with incomprehension. Helstone's advice is to '"put all crotchets out of your head and run away and amuse yourself." "What with? My doll?" asked Caroline to herself as she quitted the room' (*S.* 163–4).

Caroline, however, is not without inner strength and resourcefulness. She takes serious stock of her situation. In particular she visits two 'old maids' in her neighbourhood and learns deeply to respect their self-denying dignity. Miss Mann 'had passed alone through protracted scenes of suffering, exercised rigid self-denial, made large sacrifices of time, money, health for those who had repaid her only by ingratitude' (*S.* 153), while Miss Ainley has made herself indispensable as a sick-visitor. Caroline perceives that the place allotted to old maids 'is to do good to others, to be helpful whenever help is wanted', and that this is 'a very convenient doctrine for the people who hold it' – but, she asks, 'Is this enough? Is it to live? Is there not a terrible hollowness, mockery, want, craving, in that existence which is given away to others, for want of something of your own to bestow it on?' (S. 149). Nevertheless she puts herself at Miss Ainley's disposal; she performs all the charitable acts deemed appropriate for single women of her class; she organizes her day like a Methodist, sewing for the 'Jew-basket', working in her garden, walking long distances to tire herself – and the regime, as even Helstone has to recognize, reduces her to 'a poor little, pale, puling chit enough' (S. 162).

All this time Caroline cannot help feeling that marriage to Robert would be her salvation, and yet this hope, forlorn enough in the circumstances, is also undercut by a narrative which offers no model of happy marriage. Helstone sees marriage as 'a piece of pure folly' in which 'a yokefellow is not a companion; he or she is a fellow-sufferer' (S. 86). Caroline's own father was a violent drunkard who mistreated his little daughter and drove his wife to leave him, entrusting Caroline to her uncle. When Caroline is reunited with her mother, she too warns her against romantic accounts of marriage: 'They are not like reality: they show you only the green tempting surface of the marsh, and give not one faithful or truthful hint of the slough underneath' (S. 319). Mr and Mrs Yorke live together with their six children but are scarcely companions, while young Rose Yorke (based on Mary Taylor) has formed her own opinion of women's lot. She sees Caroline's life as 'a long, slow death', and for herself refuses to live 'a black trance like the toad's, buried in marble' or prisoned 'in the linen-press to find shrouds among the sheets' (S. 335–6).

Caroline's decline occupies most of *Shirley*'s first volume; only in its last chapter does hope appear in the shape of Shirley Keeldar herself. Shirley is Charlotte Brontë's attempt at a utopian woman: she is beautiful, vividly alive, imaginative and clever, self-confident and rich. Like Caroline, she is an orphan, but her situation is entirely different. At 21 she is independent of her guardian and has taken possession of Fieldhead, her Jacobean mansion, and its landed estate, which includes Hollow's Mill. The two young women become friends and Caroline seems, for the time being, saved from the 'barren stagnation' which threatened her life (S. 158).

'Shirley' is now such a common name for women that its impact on Charlotte's first readers is quite lost. Before Charlotte's novel, 'Shirley' was only an aristocratic surname; it is as if Charlotte had called her heiress not 'Diana' but 'Spencer' – or, indeed, 'Currer', 'Ellis' or 'Acton'. Although Shirley plays at being 'Captain Keeldar', and defies propriety by whistling and lying on the hearth-rug, she is not an unfeminine figure but a woman freed from some conventional restraints. Charlotte told Gaskell that Shirley was her effort 'to depict ... what Emily Brontë would have been, had she been placed in health and prosperity' (G. 315), and although people who knew Emily did not recognize her in Shirley's vivacious, talkative, sociable character, Shirley does also share Emily's peculiar, iconoclastic and visionary frame of mind (S. 326). Early in 1848 Charlotte wrote to Williams that 'in some points I consider Ellis [Emily] somewhat of a theorist: now and then he broaches ideas which strike my sense as much more daring and original than practical' (L. ii. 28), and as Shirley enters the novel, its conceptual horizons seem to lift. Not only does she challenge conventional ideas of womanhood – 'half doll, half angel' (S. 296) – but she focuses the novel's dissatisfaction with conventional religion.

'God save it! God also reform it!' is the narrator's ambiguous response to the Church of England (S. 254). The three curates are a disgrace, and of the three parsons depicted, only the mild and charitable Mr Hall is wholly admirable. In the mock-heroic confrontation in Volume ii, chapter 6 the dissenters are routed by the Sunday-school procession singing, not a hymn, but 'Rule, Britannia' (S. 256). Caroline and Shirley absent themselves from the church service which follows the School Feast, and Shirley broaches what Stevie Davies has called 'Emily Brontë's joyous literary feud with Milton',[14] arguing that Milton's Eve is not the first woman, but 'his cook'. Instead, in an extraordinary conflation – what Caroline calls 'a hash of Scripture and mythology' – Shirley imagines 'a woman-Titan'; Adam's equal, 'face to face she speaks with God' (S. 270–1). More remarkable, perhaps, is the fact that when Joe Scott, Robert Moore's foreman, patronizes them with St Paul's dicta, beginning 'Let the woman learn in silence, with all subjection', it is Caroline who dares answer him by citing the instability of biblical translation: 'I dare say, if I could read the original Greek...it would be possible...to give the passage quite a contrary turn; to make it say, "Let the woman speak out whenever she sees fit to make an objection"' (S. 277–8).

In that same letter to Williams, Charlotte made the rather surprising observation that 'Ellis will not be seen in his full strength till he is seen as an essayist' (L. ii. 28), and accordingly, the third volume of this novel offers us an essay by Shirley. Written as a French *devoir*, like those that Charlotte and Emily wrote for M. Heger, the essay is entitled 'The First Blue-Stocking' and describes a solitary orphan girl, at the dawn of history, whose lament reads like a mythical version of Caroline's: 'was she thus to burn out and perish, her living light doing no good, never seen, never needed...?' (S. 407). With the same epigraph as Byron's visionary verse drama, 'Heaven and Earth' (1821), however, Shirley's vision ends, like his, with the daughter of earth being rescued by a Son of God named 'Genius'. Although the essay's mythical mode is unlike anything Emily wrote, its ideas thus recall Emily's poems to the 'God within my breast', or the 'Invisible' visitant of 'The Prisoner'.[15] Most modern readers find the essay embarrassing, especially as all five pages are improbably rehearsed from memory by Shirley's ex-tutor, Louis Moore. Lyndall Gordon, however, points out that Shirley's 'parable sets up a model for the feminist parables, called *Dreams*, which Olive Schreiner published in 1891' and which inspired the suffragettes.[16]

Visionary and utopian writing tends to appear when the practical obstacles to progress are daunting, and although Shirley playfully assumes a masculine freedom of behaviour, in essentials she is not free. Like Caroline, she wishes for 'a profession – a trade' (S. 193), and even her attempts to dispense charity need masculine approval. Volume ii, chapter 3 ends with 'Captain Keeldar...radiant with glee' (S. 231) at having charmed the three rectors into endorsing her plans, but she has worked through 'women's influence' rather than direct power.

The most dramatic demonstration of the women's marginality comes in Volume ii, chapter 8, when Caroline and Shirley are alone together at the Rectory. Hearing the tramp of hundreds of men passing the house at midnight, they run across the fields to Hollow's Mill to warn Robert. They are too late; moreover, Robert has defended his mill with soldiers and the attack is beaten off. The women can do nothing but look on from an invisible vantage point. Their impotence is highlighted by contrast with Gaskell's later industrial novel, *North and South* (1854–5), which appears to quote key words from *Shirley* in a pointed riposte. While Shirley and Caroline contemplate intervention – 'a romantic rush onto the stage' – they 'both knew they would do no good by rushing down into the mêlée' (*S.* 289, 290). Gaskell's heroine, Margaret, however, does intervene, and despite her personal shame at having thrown herself 'into the mêlée, like a romantic fool!', she later decides that she 'did some good', not only defending the beleaguered manufacturer, but also preventing the workers from committing further crimes.[17]

Gaskell's more optimistic scenario derives from a personal and social situation very different from Charlotte Brontë's. Not only was she a happily married woman, surrounded by family, friends and a rich cultural milieu, she was also a member of the forward-looking Unitarian Church, which believed in equal education for women and in the achievability of progress through human reason and compassion. Charlotte Brontë's more fatalistic position derived not only from her conservative outlook, but also from her personal experience. The first volume of *Shirley* was written during the spring and summer of 1848, while Branwell's state continued to deteriorate; in September he died, from chronic bronchitis exacerbated by abuse of opium and alcohol. Worse was to follow: in December Emily died of tuberculosis, refusing to the last day to acknowledge her illness. 'Moments so dark as these I have never known', wrote Charlotte (*L.* ii. 154). During the spring of 1849 she limped ahead with Volume ii of *Shirley*, but now Anne was failing and she too died, of tuberculosis, in May. Amazingly, Charlotte returned to the work and finished Volume iii in August.

This appalling series of bereavements has been used by critics to account for *Shirley*'s structural weakness and unevenness of tone. These deaths had, however, a more precise effect on the novel's general outlook. Of Branwell, Charlotte wrote, 'I do not weep from a sense of bereavement... but for the wreck of talent, the ruin of promise, the untimely, dreary extinction of what might have been a burning and a shining light' (*L.* ii. 122). Emily 'has died in a time of promise – we saw her torn from life in its prime' (*L.* ii. 157). Anne, as she neared death, wrote that

> I hoped amid the brave and strong
> My portioned task might lie,
> To toil amid the labouring throng
> With purpose pure and high.[18]

She felt that the 'hope of life' was taken from her before she had achieved her aims. The repeated lament is of hope blighted, talents wasted, human endeavour frustrated, and it is this failure of hope which colours the novel's conclusions, both public and private, creating a dark counterpoint to the era's more general social optimism.

Despite the novel's pleas for the employment of women, and its negative picture of marriage, marriage was the best outcome that Charlotte could envisage for her heroines ('you are a coward & a traitor', wrote Mary Taylor from her New Zealand shop (*L.* ii. 392)). There is a splendidly comic scene (Volume iii, chapter 8) in which Shirley defies her uncle's claim to dictate whom she marries, but this is followed by a painfully long-drawn-out negotiation between a half-reluctant Shirley and her chosen mate, Robert's brother, Louis (Volume iii, chapter 13). Although Louis occupies the lowly position of tutor in her uncle's family, he is a tall, strong, sensitive, self-possessed and decisive man. He proves well fitted to be master of Fieldhead, and even to be master of Shirley (as she says she wishes), but once 'fettered to a fixed day', 'she pined, like any other chained denizen of deserts' (*S.* 534). Meanwhile Robert Moore, like Mr Rochester, is chastened by experience. Mortified by his own treachery in proposing a mercenary marriage to Shirley, and by her furious refusal, he leaves for London where he sees the sufferings of the poor at closer quarters (*S.* 453–4). Shot, on his return, by the crazed weaver, he learns what it is to be sick and dependent on the care of others. Caroline accepts his proposal as the answer to her dreams, but the context of their marriage is muted.

Volume iii, begun almost immediately after Anne's death, had opened with a chapter entitled 'The Valley of the Shadow of

Death', as Caroline, alone and hopeless once more as she imagines that Shirley will marry Robert, sinks into a fever, and there is no mistaking the authentic voice of agony as Mrs Pryor, revealed as Caroline's mother, struggles for her recovery (S. 369). Again, however, the import of this chapter is not one of simple grief. Early in 1849 Charlotte and Anne read one of Anne's poems which had been printed in *Fraser's Magazine*; immediately before it was the last instalment of Charles Kingsley's social-problem novel, *Yeast* (1848–9). Kingsley's last chapter is also entitled 'The Valley of the Shadow of Death', but as Heather Glen points out, Kingsley the Christian Socialist ends his novel with

> a progressive vision of a 'nobler, more chivalrous, more god-like' England – of 'railroads, electric telegraphs, associate lodging-houses, club-houses, sanitary reforms, experimental schools, chemical agriculture, a matchless school of inductive science ... – and all this in the very workshop of the world!'[19]

Charlotte's conclusion is different.

The title of *Shirley*'s last chapter, 'The Winding-up', blatantly announces its fictionality, and by contrast with Kingsley seems to mock our expectations. The heroines are married in a sentence like a newspaper small-ad. (S. 541), while the long-awaited repeal of the Orders in Council descends on the scene with risible rapidity, like the *deus ex machina* in a Greek play: 'warehouses were lightened, ships were laden, work abounded, wages rose: the good time seemed come' (S. 534). The vision of the future which Robert offers to Caroline is, moreover, curiously heartless, given her attachment to the landscape:

> 'the copse shall be firewood ere five years elapse: the beautiful wild ravine shall be a smooth descent; the green natural terrace shall be a paved street: there shall be cottages in the dark ravine, and cottages on the lonely slopes: the rough pebbled track shall be an even, firm, broad, black, sooty road, bedded with cinders from my mill: and my mill, Caroline – my mill shall fill its present yard.' (S. 540)

It is as if the utopian vision of 1812 is unveiled as the nightmare of 1849.

The last paragraphs of the novel hark back to a time before the mill, when the Hollow was the haunt of fairies, and while *Jane Eyre*'s invocations of fairies remain playful, here they suggest a lament for a lost, pre-industrial past, reminding us that throughout this odd, tragic, caustic novel there are passages of great beauty, never ironized or overcast with acrimony, picturing the landscape, the seasons and the weather. Trees dappled with sunshine or roaring like an ocean in tempest, uplands humming with bees or livid with impending storm, becks musical, turbulent or glacially still, the green Hollow safely embowering or dark with menace, sunsets resplendent or lurid, winds laden with Eastern contagion or fresh with spring renewal, gardens luscious with colour or dank with winter decay, night skies starlit, moonlit, clouded or dark midnight blue – in the strange patchwork of *Shirley* these descriptions gleam like jewels. Far more than her strained attempt to capture her sister's philosophy, Charlotte's evocations of the natural world stand as her memorial to Emily's love of mother earth, and as her own best claim to being a poet.

5

Villette

I tore her up – the incubus! I held her on high – the goblin! I shook
her loose – the mystery! And down she fell – down all round me –
down in shreds and fragments – and I trode upon her. (*V.* 470)

Villette has never been as popular as *Jane Eyre* – Kate Millett
describes it as 'too subversive to be popular'[1] – but its critical
reputation is perhaps even higher. George Eliot found it 'a still
more wonderful book than *Jane Eyre*', with 'something almost
preternatural in its power'.[2] The modern critics Sandra Gilbert
and Susan Gubar are characteristically uncompromising:

> Lucy Snowe, *Villette*'s protagonist-narrator, older and wiser than any
> of Brontë's other heroines, is from first to last a woman *without* –
> outside society, without parents or friends, without physical or
> mental attractions, without money or confidence or health – and her
> story is perhaps the most moving and terrifying account of female
> deprivation ever written.[3]

The Victorian feminist Harriet Martineau found the book
'almost intolerably painful', afflicting the reader 'with an
amount of subjective misery which we may fairly remonstrate
against'.[4] Matthew Arnold agreed, disliking the book because
'the writer's mind contains nothing but hunger, rebellion and
rage'.[5]

For modern feminists, however, Charlotte Brontë's tale of
emotional hunger is a valuable and necessary exposure of an
important reality, and Arnold's phrase about 'hunger, rebellion
and rage' has become a rallying-cry for protest against the
constraints of conventional femininity. Although Gilbert and
Gubar call *Villette* 'Charlotte Brontë's most overtly and despair-
ingly feminist novel',[6] Kate Millett emphasizes the power which
resists the despair. For her, the heroine of *Villette* is a 'neurotic

revolutionary full of conflict, back-sliding, anger, terrible self-doubt, and an unconquerable determination to win through'. Lucy may be imprisoned by her society, but, Millett writes, 'escape is all over the book; *Villette* reads like one long meditation on a prison break'.[7]

If *Villette* is primarily a study of interiority, of psychological isolation, however, this is not defined, as in *Jane Eyre* and *Shirley*, by geographical remoteness from 'the busy world, towns, regions full of life' (*JE* 109). Instead, Lucy's story unfolds in an urban and densely material social context, and this strange conjunction, as Heather Glen demonstrates, derives partly from Charlotte Brontë's own experience during the years of the novel's composition.[8] More than three years elapsed between the publication of *Shirley* in October 1849, and that of *Villette* in January 1853. The daily pattern of Charlotte's life in these years was radically changed by the deaths of her brother and sisters in 1848–9 which, given her father's reclusive habits, left her effectively alone in the Parsonage at Haworth. The silence and solitude, intensified by her recollection of her sisters' habitual companionship, was sometimes more than she could bear.

In 1850 Charlotte undertook to write a 'Biographical Notice of Ellis and Acton Bell' to accompany a new edition of *Wuthering Heights* and *Agnes Grey*. Now that Emily and Anne were dead there seemed no reason to maintain these pseudonyms, and Charlotte includes many details of their lives, with the emotional colouring which did so much to shape 'the Brontë myth'. For Charlotte, this writing 'brought back the pang of bereavement and occasioned a depression of spirits well nigh intolerable – for one or two nights I scarcely knew how to get on till morning – and when morning came I was still haunted with a sense of sickening distress' (*L.* ii. 487). Elsewhere she refers to this state as 'hypochondria', a word which then meant not imaginary suffering but something more like clinical depression.[9] The experience was not new; as early as 1846 she had described a feeling of 'concentrated anguish' which clothed existence in 'preternatural horror far worse than [being] buried... in a subterranean dungeon' (*L.* i 505). This imagery of burial, already prominent in *Shirley*, becomes dominant in *Villette*.

Despite her efforts to be stoical, Charlotte sometimes felt an absolute necessity to get away from Haworth, to see new faces and absorb new ideas, and her publisher, George Smith, was happy to receive Charlotte in the London home which he shared with his mother and sisters for a number of visits in 1849–52. Charlotte had already met Smith in July 1848, when she and Anne travelled to London to scotch rumours that 'Currer', 'Ellis' and 'Acton' Bell were only one person. At that time only George Smith and his reader, William Smith Williams, were let into the secret of their identity, but after the publication of *Shirley*, Charlotte's incognito was gradually eroded, and she was appalled at the idea of being 'lionised', or treated as a literary celebrity. Guarded by George Smith, however, she visited art galleries, museums, notable preachers, literary lectures and theatres, and in 1851 she made five visits to the Great Exhibition at the Crystal Palace. The Great Exhibition, designed to bring together artefacts and inventions from throughout the British Empire, was an impressive experience and Charlotte described it to her father as 'like a mighty Vanity Fair – the brightest colours blaze on all sides – and ware of all kinds – from diamonds to spinning jennies and Printing Presses are there to be seen – It was very fine – gorgeous – animated – bewildering – but I liked Thackeray's lecture better' (*L*. ii. 625).

George Smith himself, young, handsome and genial, was a major element in her enjoyment of these visits, and letters between Charlotte and Ellen Nussey hint at a warmer feeling than friendship. Late in 1852, when Charlotte submitted the half-written manuscript of *Villette* for Smith's approval, he recognized himself in the character of Dr John, and Charlotte in Lucy Snowe, and their relationship became curiously entwined with the novel's progress. While its outcome was still uncertain, Charlotte wrote to Smith that 'Lucy must not marry Dr John; he is far too youthful, handsome, bright-spirited and sweet-tempered' (*L*. iii. 77–8). Although Juliet Barker speculates that Smith himself might have contemplated marriage with Charlotte, it is probable that Charlotte's own assessment is the accurate one (B. 836).

George Smith, however, was not Charlotte's only host. In August 1850 she stayed with Sir James Kay Shuttleworth, the social reformer, at his holiday house in the Lake District, where she met the novelist Elizabeth Gaskell. The two women immediately liked one another and Gaskell was later to become

Charlotte's biographer. A more surprising friend was the free-thinking essayist and novelist Harriet Martineau, with whom Charlotte stayed, again in the Lake District, in December 1850. One result of these encounters was that Charlotte lost some of her deference towards the critics. She had already had some friendly correspondence with George Henry Lewes, but when Lewes abused her confidence by reviewing *Shirley* specifically as the product of a childless woman, she had replied in one sentence: 'I can be on my guard against my enemies, but God deliver me from my friends!' (*L*. ii. 330). When she met Lewes six months later, he again offered an insensitive comment, and George Smith reports witnessing for the first time 'the fire concealed beneath her mildness', listening 'with mingled admiration and alarm to the indignant eloquence with which his impertinent remark was answered' (quoted B. 757). Charlotte berated Thackeray in a similar way for having carelessly revealed her identity in a public place. As Smith reports, 'the spectacle of this little woman, hardly reaching to Thackeray's elbow, but, somehow, looking stronger and fiercer than himself, and casting her incisive words at his head, resembled the dropping of shells into a fortress' (quoted B. 798).

The excitement of visits and meetings always, however, left Charlotte exhausted and ill, with sick headaches and depression, plunging her back into the state she likened to that of 'the prisoner in solitary confinement – the toad in the block of marble' (*L*. ii 232). After Anne's death she had turned to her work on *Shirley* to help her through the bleak days, but now, 'caught up in this cycle of intolerable self-consciousness in public and intolerable loneliness in private, of compulsive assertion and withdrawal, her writing faltered'.[10] She tried to begin a new novel early in 1850, but she made no progress, and a year later, conscious of her obligation to Smith, Elder, she tried again to interest them in *The Professor*. When they again politely declined, she began to think of a new use for her Brussels experiences, and *Villette* was slowly written in 1851–2.[11]

It is a mistake, however, to see *Villette* as a 'reworking' of *The Professor*. Like the earlier novel, *Villette* is largely set in a Pensionnat, or girls' school, in a fictional version of Brussels, and the female directors of these schools are similar in character, but there are few other parallels. The major difference is that *Villette* has a female first-person narrator. Like Jane Eyre, Lucy Snowe is an orphan, thrown on her own devices, and she makes her living first as companion to an invalid lady and then, after an audacious voyage alone across the channel, as a nursery governess and later as a teacher in the town called 'Villette' in the country called 'Labassecour' – fictionalized versions of Brussels and Belgium. Like Jane Eyre, Lucy has two possible lovers – the fair, handsome, cheerful Dr John Graham Bretton, and the dark, intense, irascible Monsieur Paul Emanuel.

Villette, however, is very far from being another *Jane Eyre*. Lucy Snowe does not, like Jane Eyre, open her heart to the reader – in fact, in the early chapters of the novel she takes pains to present herself as merely a colourless observer of other people's lives. She is at this time 'a child', but her behaviour is not child-like, and her age is indeterminate (although it is possible to work out later that she is about 13). She is not at home, but on a visit to her godmother, Mrs Bretton, and we learn nothing about her 'permanent residence' except that it is not with parents but with 'kinsfolk' (*V.* 5). If readers choose to imagine that she was 'glad to return to the bosom of my kindred' she will not contradict 'the amiable conjecture'. In fact, in a narrative strategy characteristic of the novel, she 'will permit the reader to picture me, for the next eight years, as a bark slumbering through halcyon weather, in a harbour still as glass.... A great many women and girls are supposed to pass their lives something in that fashion; why not I with the rest?'

In a novel heavily reliant on metaphor for suggesting states of mind and body, such 'imagining' is persuasively offered to the reader, only to be shattered in the next paragraph:

> However, it cannot be concealed that, in that case, I must somehow have fallen over-board, or that there must have been wreck at last. I too well remember a time – a long time, of cold, of danger, of contention. To this hour, when I have the nightmare, it repeats the rush and saltiness of briny waves in my throat, and their icy pressure on my lungs. I even know there was a storm, and that not of one hour nor one day. For many days and nights neither sun nor stars appeared; we cast with our own hands the tackling out of the ship; a heavy tempest lay on us; all hope that we should be saved was taken away. In fine, the ship was lost, the crew perished.

Again, the biblical intensity of the metaphor leaves us uncertain whether this is a real shipwreck[12] until, in the next paragraph, Lucy reports laconically that 'as far as I recollect, I complained to no-one about these troubles'. She goes on to tell us that she now, in fact, had no-one to complain to, since she had lost contact even with Mrs Bretton (*V.* 35).

By chapter 4, therefore, Lucy is not only an orphan but 'there remained no possibility of dependence on others; to myself alone could I look' (*V.* 36). Her position as companion to an invalid lady offers a 'little morsel of human affection, which I prized as if it were a solid pearl', but this is lost when Miss Marchmont suddenly dies. It seems that she must 'be goaded, driven, stung, forced to energy' (*V.* 38), and it is under this impetus, acting on the chance remark of an acquaintance, that she braves the journey to Villette. While crossing the channel, she meets Ginevra Fanshawe, who later appears as a pupil at the school where Lucy is employed, and a narrative pattern begins to emerge: Lucy may not have a clear goal for her own life, but she is continually observing those of other girls and women.

In the first three chapters Lucy is preoccupied by the behaviour of Polly Home, a younger girl who comes to stay with Mrs Bretton. This diminutive 6-year-old apes conventional feminine behaviour, hemming handkerchieves, carrying tea-cups, and endlessly solicitous of the comfort of menfolk. Separated from her beloved papa, she 'mope[s]' (*V.* 12) until Mrs Bretton's teenage son, John Graham, becomes a new object of devotion. Faced with separation from Graham, she suffers 'dedful miz-er-y!' (*V.* 32), leaving Lucy to wonder 'how will she get through this world, or battle with this life?' (*V.* 34). In Miss Marchmont, we see a possible adult version of little Polly, 'a woe-struck and selfish woman' who has spent thirty years mourning the loss of her lover (*V.* 41). Ginevra, by contrast, as one of a numerous shabby-genteel family, knows that she must make the most of her good looks to marry someone with money (*V.* 55), and is undeterred by the spectacle of another girl who has just made such a match to the 'oldest, plainest, greasiest, broadest' man in a 'fat, and vulgar' group (*V.* 52).

Each of these girls and women takes it for granted that her destiny lies in the hands of men, who have the power to confer love, security and wealth, and later in Lucy's life she finds that men have complementary assumptions. At an exhibition, she sees a painting of Cleopatra, which is described by some young men as 'le type du voluptueux' (*V*. 206) – in other words, the sort of woman that men desire – while Lucy provides the mocking valuation of realism, describing her as 'strong enough to do the work of two plain cooks' (*V*. 200). Dr John, on the other hand, makes 'a branding judgment' of the actress Vashti (*V*. 260), while for Lucy, Vashti has 'power like a deep, swollen, winter river, thundering in cataract, and bearing the soul, like a leaf, on the steep and steely sweep of its descent' (*V*. 259). Most telling of all is the series of paintings representing the typical woman, as a young girl, a bride, a young mother and a widow. For Lucy, they are 'cold and vapid as ghosts. What women to live with! insincere, ill-humoured, bloodless, brainless nonentities!' (*V*. 202).

To begin with, it seems that Lucy has abstracted herself from this male-female economy in which women depend on, and submit to being judged by, men. In observing Polly's emotion, she insists that 'I, Lucy Snowe, was calm' (*V*. 22), and in contrast to Ginevra's plans she declares that 'my business is to earn a living where I can find it' (*V*. 55). In some ways she admires Mme Beck, the director of the school where she comes to be employed. A widow with three daughters, Mme Beck owns and manages a large and profitable establishment. Through a system of espionage, she controls both pupils and teachers while appearing calm, bland and benign. Lucy soon discovers, however, that Mme Beck's independence is circumscribed by social and religious expectations. Her pupils' parents, and above all the Catholic Church, expect that the girls should be kept 'in blind ignorance, and under a surveillance that left them no moment and no corner for retirement' (*V*. 73).

Although Lucy is at first amused to find this 'surveillance' practised on her, she soon rebels at the ideology which underlies it. Every evening, the resident pupils must listen to legends of the saints, including 'the dread boasts of confessors, who had wickedly abused their office' – stories like that of 'Elizabeth of Hungary... with all its dreadful viciousness, sickening tyranny and black impiety: tales that were nightmares of oppression, privation, and agony' (*V*. 117). Charlotte had been deeply affected by the story of Elizabeth of Hungary as told by Charles Kingsley in *The Saint's Tragedy* (1848) (*L*. ii. 677),[13] and in

1850 her growing anti-Catholic alarm was matched by a more general 'hysterical reaction' to what was perceived as 'papal aggression', when the Pope appointed Nicholas Wiseman as Cardinal and Archbishop of Westminster, thus presenting for the first time since the reformation an institutional challenge to the Church of England (B. 781).

Charlotte Brontë's anger was fuelled specifically by the Catholic practice of confession, and by the Church's resulting power to crush individual liberty of conscience. In his book, *Discipline and Punish* (1975), Michel Foucault argues that during the nineteenth century surveillance took the place of institutional force as the primary mode of controlling populations, and, as Sally Shuttleworth points out, *Villette*, 'with its obsessional concern with surveillance, fits almost too perfectly into the paradigm' outlined by Foucault. Foucault takes as his controlling metaphor Jeremy Bentham's 1791 'Panopticon', a plan for a model prison in which inmates could at all times be surveyed by a single warder – a system which, as Shuttleworth says, 'might describe the underlying nightmare of *Villette* from which Lucy is for ever trying to escape'.[14]

From the outset Lucy's refusal to reveal herself seems a matter of self-preservation. As she plans her audacious voyage to Villette, she notes that 'I had a staid manner of my own which ere now had been as good to me as cloak and hood of hodden gray, since under its favour I had been enabled to achieve with impunity, and even approbation, deeds that if attempted with an excited and unsettled air, would in some minds have stamped me as a dreamer and a zealot' (*V.* 44). In Mme Beck's school, where 'no corner was sacred from intrusion, where not a tear could be shed, nor a thought pondered, but a spy was at hand to note and to divine' (*V.* 231), Lucy seeks privacy in a neglected part of the school garden where, according to legend, a nun had been buried alive by 'a monkish conclave of the drear middle ages ... for some sin against her vow'. The nun's ghost is said to haunt the garden, and although Lucy at first dismisses the story as 'romantic rubbish' (*V.* 106), the figure of the nun becomes a crucial symbol of female life nullified by priestly control.

Ghostly nuns were a stock-in-trade of the sensational Gothic novels of the late eighteenth century which the Brontë sisters would have met through popular journals of their own time. In *Villette*, however, Charlotte Brontë uses the clichéd motif in a new and disturbing way. When the nun begins to appear to Lucy, it seems a supernatural phenomenon. This 'ghost', however, appears at moments of Lucy's psychological tension, encouraging the interpretation favoured by Dr John, that it is a 'case of spectral illusion' (*V.* 249), a hallucination. The real explanation proves to be rational and material: the 'ghost' is Ginevra Fanshawe's lover in the disguise he uses to visit her. The three explanations are incompatible, yet they all persist until near the end as simultaneous impossibilities in Lucy's evasive narrative. The striking thing is that the haunting is so managed as to enhance the psychological depth of the novel without damaging its credibility in realist terms. Robert Heilman thus argues that 'Charlotte Brontë's "New" Gothic' gives 'dramatic form to impulses and feelings which, because of their depth or mysteriousness or intensity or ambiguity, or of their ignoring or transcending everyday norms of propriety or reason, increase wonderfully the sense of reality in the novel'.[15]

Decisive cracks in Lucy's 'calm' persona appear at the end of the novel's first volume, when she is left alone in the school during the long vacation, and experiences solitude so intense as to bring 'mental pain'. She describes how her 'want of companionship maintained in my soul the cravings of a most deadly famine' (*V.* 158), and in this extreme need reaches what Shuttleworth calls 'the nadir of her mental state':[16] she makes a confession to a Catholic priest. The beginning of Volume ii, however, sees her rescued from priestly menace. After fainting from exhaustion, she revives in what seems a reproduction of the Bretton house. It emerges that Dr John, who has figured for several chapters as a physician at the school, is no other than John Graham Bretton, now living in Villette with his mother. Moreover, Lucy tells us that she recognized him some time back but 'to *hint* at my discovery, had not suited my habits of thought' (*V.* 175). This apparently perverse concealment can, in the context, be read as Lucy's assertion of control over knowledge which she can hide from others.

Now begins a new phase of Lucy's life, in which Dr John (like George Smith for Charlotte Brontë) escorts her to places of entertainment and art, and it is notable that despite the

71

minutely registered material luxury of these scenes, they appear hardly more solid and reassuring than her ghostly fantasies. As Heather Glen points out, 'again and again in the novel, the image recurs of the eye less as organizing than as simply receiving impressions, of a world that baffles, bewilders, dazzles, strikes'.[17] In the concert hall, for instance,

> pendant from the dome, flamed a mass that dazzled me – a mass, I thought, of rock-crystal, sparkling with facets, streaming with drops, ablaze with stars, and gorgeously tinged with dews of gems dissolved, or fragments of rainbows shivered. It was only the chandelier, reader, but for me it seemed the work of eastern genii: I almost looked to see if a huge, dark cloudy hand – that of the Slave of the Lamp – were not hovering in the lustrous and perfumed atmosphere of the cupola, guarding its wondrous treasure. (V. 209)

When Lucy returns to school, Dr John (again like George Smith) relieves the blankness of her life with letters which become essential to her well-being. It is her overwrought anticipation of pleasure from the first of these letters which seems to invite the first apparition of the nun in the attic of the school, where she has sought solitude to read it. In describing her longing for the human contact represented by the letters she uses metaphors of starvation, of burial and of solitary confinement which sends the prisoner mad (V. 273) – metaphors which clearly link her with the nun's story, especially when, in her panic at seeing the nun, she drops her letter, and in searching for it becomes a 'grovelling, groping, monomaniac' (V. 246).

This intense emotion is not unheralded. From quite early in the novel the 'calm' Lucy, who pleads 'guiltless of that curse, an overheated and discursive imagination', reveals herself not only as so susceptible to little Polly's emotion that she feels 'haunted' by it (V. 12), but also as strangely affected by stormy weather, which 'woke the being I was always lulling, and stirred up a craving cry I could not satisfy'. In one extraordinary passage she describes how she sits on the window-ledge outside her bedroom window in the school, unable to 'go in: too resistless was the delight of staying with the wild hour, black and full of thunder, pealing out such an ode as language never delivered to man – too terribly glorious, the spectacle of clouds, split and pierced by white and blinding bolts' (V. 109). The emotion is not, however, reciprocal. Dr John's reaction to Vashti makes Lucy realize that 'for what belonged to storm, what was wild and intense, dangerous, sudden, and flaming, he had no sympathy' (*V.* 259). Moreover, after five letters his attention shifts from Lucy to little Polly who, in a further improbable coincidence, re-emerges as a grown-up Paulina de Bassompierre. In a chapter entitled 'A Burial', Lucy buries his letters, choosing the very place where the nun is supposed to be entombed – and the nun again appears (*V.* 296–7).

Towards the end of Volume i, we are introduced to M. Paul Emanuel, a cousin of Mme Beck and a visiting teacher at the school. Lucy's description of 'a dark little man' with 'his close-shorn, black head, his broad, sallow brow, his thin cheek, his wide and quivering nostril, his thorough glance and hurried bearing' (*V.* 129), recalls Charlotte's description of her teacher, M. Heger, 'a little, black, ugly being with a face that varies in expression' (*L.* i. 284), who was nevertheless the only man who thoroughly recognized her ability and force of character. By contrast with Lucy's determined self-suppression, M. Paul is 'a species of whirlwind' (*V.* 135) who fumes 'like a bottled storm' (*V.* 154), and where other people are deceived by her manner, thinking 'that a colourless shadow has gone by' (*V.* 155), his opinion is 'that mine was rather a fiery and rash nature – adventurous, indocile, and audacious' (*V.* 301). Throughout Volume ii, as Dr John recedes from Lucy's life, M. Paul becomes more important, and he dominates Volume iii to the point where she acknowledges that 'his mind was indeed my library, and whenever it was opened to me, I entered bliss' (*V.* 381).

In her review of *Villette*, Harriet Martineau objects to the fact that

> all the female characters, in all their thoughts and lives, are full of one thing... – love... and, so dominant is this idea – so incessant is the writer's tendency to describe the need of being loved, that the heroine... leaves the reader at last under the uncomfortable impression of her having either entertained a double love, or allowed one to supersede another without notification of the transition.[18]

Despite the intensity of Lucy's attachment to Dr John, however, she disclaims, 'with the utmost scorn, every sneaking suspicion of what are called "warmer feelings"' on the ground that it is 'mortal absurdity' to launch into Love without Hope (*V.* 254).

Even if we suspect that the lady doth protest too much, it is clear that her need of him arises from loneliness. In a letter to Ellen Nussey, Charlotte Brontë is precise: 'The evils that now and then wring a groan from my heart – lie in position – not that I am a *single* woman and likely to remain a *single* woman – but because I am a *lonely* woman and likely to be *lonely*' (*L*. iii. 63). By contrast with Dr John, Lucy is drawn to M. Paul because he shares with her that 'chord for enthusiasm' which Dr John lacks (*V*. 259). Even his Catholic beliefs are not a barrier to their friendship or even to their marriage, because 'all Rome could not put into him bigotry... He was born honest, and not false – artless, and not cunning – a freeman, and not a slave' (*V*. 494). The real barrier is his entanglement with the institutions and obligations of that Church, which extends over them both 'the surveillance of a sleepless eye' (*V*. 409). It is here that the image of the nun gathers further reverberations.

M. Paul is Mme Beck's cousin, and if she cannot marry him herself she is determined that he should not marry the Protestant Lucy. In this, she is aided by the very Catholic priest, Père Silas, who heard Lucy's confession, and who now proves to be M. Paul's spiritual mentor. Behind them both is the grotesque figure of Mme Walravens, the grandmother of Justine Marie, once beloved of M. Paul. Prevented by her parents from marrying him, Justine Marie took the veil and died, and when Lucy visits Mme Walravens in chapter 34, the old woman appears to walk into the room through a portrait of Justine Marie as a nun. The coincidences and uncanny setting of this chapter are blatant in their fantastic resonances, as Lucy the narrator recognizes. 'Hoar enchantment here prevailed; a spell had opened for me elf-land – that cell-like room, that vanishing picture, that arch and passage, and stair of stone, were all parts of a fairy tale. Distincter even than these scenic details stood the chief figure – Cunégonde, the sorceress – Malevola, the evil fairy' (*V*. 389). As the old woman leaves, 'a peal of thunder broke, and a flash of lightning blazed broad over salon and boudoir. The tale of magic seemed to proceed with due accompaniment of the elements. The wanderer, decoyed into the enchanted castle, heard rising, outside, the spell-wakened tempest' (*V*. 389–90).

Lucy's half-mocking words, which create an uncanny atmosphere at the same time that they appear to undercut it, are in

74

tune with her general evasiveness, which refuses to provide clear boundaries by which the reader can distinguish reality from fantasy, or learn the value of either. In chapter 21, for instance, when Lucy returns to school after her idyll with Dr John, she castigates Reason (or realism) as a hag who has 'turned me out by night, in mid-winter, on cold snow, flinging for sustenance the gnawed bone dogs had forsaken', while Imagination has assuaged her hunger with heavenly manna, 'food, sweet and strange, gathered amongst gleaning angels' (*V.* 229–30). A few pages later, however, she longs 'deliriously for natural and earth-grown food' instead of 'a mess of that manna I drearily eulogized awhile ago... which, in the end, our souls full surely loathe' (*V.* 239).

In her essay, 'The Buried Letter', the feminist critic Mary Jacobus quotes Freud's famous essay on 'The Uncanny', pointing out that it

> offers a classic formulation of Gothic strategy: 'the writer creates a kind of uncertainly in us... by not letting us know, no doubt purposely, whether he is taking us into the real world or into a purely fantastic one of his own creation'. The effect of this uncertainty in Charlotte Brontë's novel is to challenge the mono-polistic claims of realism on 'reality' – to render its representation no less fictive and arbitrary than the Gothic and Romantic modes.[19]

The most striking examples of this narrative uncertainty are found in chapters 38 and 39, when Lucy, driven to her wits' end by being separated from M. Paul on the eve of his departure for Guadaloupe, escapes from the school and, under the influence of drugs administered by Mme Beck, seeks to walk in the park at midnight. There she finds, not the cool refreshment she expected, but

> a land of enchantment, a garden most gorgeous, a plain sprinkled with coloured meteors, a forest with sparks of purple and ruby and golden fire gemming the foliage; a region, not of trees and shadow, but of strangest architectural wealth – of altar and of temple, of pyramid, obelisk, and sphynx; incredible to say, the wonders and the symbols of Egypt teemed throughout the park of Villette.

Lucy even comments on her own double vision: 'no matter that I quickly recognized the material of these solemn fragments – the timber, the paint, and the paste-board – these inevitable discoveries failed to quite destroy the charm, or undermine the marvel of that night' (*V.* 453). More important is that Lucy's double vision extends to her evaluation of motives. In a further theatrical coincidence, she finds gathered together in the phantasmagoric scene first her English friends, the Brettons and de Bassompierres, and then, more dramatically, the 'junta' of Mme Beck, Père Silas and Mme Walravens (*V.* 460), who are then joined by M. Paul and a young girl called Justine Marie. The name brings before Lucy 'the pictured nun ... the vision of the garret, the apparition of the alley', and she asks, 'when imagination once runs riot where do we stop? What winter tree so bare and branchless ... that Fancy ... will not clothe it in spirituality, and make of it a phantom?' Here, she invokes the uncanny only to destroy it. In the strange atmosphere of the park,

> scarce would you discredit me, reader, were I to say that she is like the nun of the attic, that she wears black skirts and white head-clothes, that she looks the resurrection of the flesh, and that she is a risen ghost.
>
> All falsities – all figments! We will not deal in this gear. Let us be honest, and cut, as heretofore, from the homely web of truth.... A girl of Villette stands there. (*V.* 463–4)

Two pages later, however, 'truth' itself deceives her. Recognizing that M. Paul's 'nun was indeed buried', Lucy persuades herself that he is engaged to this current Justine Marie. 'Thus it must be. The revelation was indeed come. Presentiment had not been mistaken ... it was I who had for a moment miscalculated; not seeing the true bearing of the oracle, I had thought she muttered of vision when, in truth, her prediction touched reality'. She refuses to weigh probabilities: 'far from me such shifts and palliatives, far from me such temporary evasion of the actual, such coward fleeing from the dread, the swift-footed, the all-overtaking Fact such traitor defection from the TRUTH'. As the final chapters show, Lucy is mistaken; M. Paul loves and wishes to marry her, but at this point she experiences two opposite responses. She believes that this 'truth' has set her free (*V.* 467), but at the same time she is attacked by an uncontrollable jealousy: 'something tore me so cruelly under my shawl, something so dug into my side, a vulture so strong in beak and talon, I must be alone to grapple with it' (*V.* 468).

It is under the influence of this unendurable emotion that she returns to the school and finds, 'stretched on my bed the old phantom – the NUN'. In this extremity, it is emotion, not thought, which motivates her: 'lashed up by a new scourge, I defied spectra. In a moment, without exclamation, I had rushed on the haunted couch; nothing leaped out, or sprung, or stirred; all the movement was mine, so was all the life, the reality, the substance, the force; as my instinct felt' (*V.* 470). Just as the actress Vashti sees pain as 'a thing that can be attacked, worried down, torn in shreds' (*V.* 258), so Lucy now declares that 'I tore her up – the incubus! I held her on high – the goblin! I shook her loose – the mystery! And down she fell – down all round me – down in shreds and fragments – and I trode upon her'. The nun is nothing but the empty robes used by Ginevra's lover – 'the branchless tree' (*V.* 470) worked on by Fancy to become a 'phantom' (*V.* 464). It is a mistake, however, to assume that this 'real' explanation negates the previous visions. As Jacobus argues, 'instead of correcting the novel into a false coherence, we should see in its ruptured and ambiguous discourse the source of its uncanny power.'[20]

Beyond this, we should see that the fictive power lies in the hand of the narrator, and that it persists to the end of the novel. When Thackeray read *Villette*, he thought that what it revealed about Charlotte Brontë was that 'rather than have fame, rather than any other earthly good or mayhap heavenly one she wants some Tomkins or another to love her and be in love with' (quoted B. 849). Gilbert and Gubar, however, rather emphasize 'Lucy's ambivalence about love and about men ...: she seeks emotional and erotic involvement as the only available form of self-actualization in her world, yet she fears such involvement will lead either to submission or to destruction, suicide or homicide'.[21] M. Paul plays the part of 'the great recognizer'; he is essential to Lucy's well-being, just as Rochester is for Jane Eyre, because he confirms and mirrors back to her her sense of self-worth. Jane Eyre conquers her apprehension about marriage and becomes 'one flesh' with her mate, but Lucy practises what Shuttleworth calls 'creative evasion' to the end.[22]

Lucy sustains the self-confidence born of destroying the nun to the point where, when Mme Beck tries physically to separate her from M. Paul, she cries out before friend and enemy that 'my heart will break!' (*V.* 481). For his part, M. Paul effectively gives Lucy her freedom in the shape of her own school, her life as well as her livelihood thereafter. More important, in place of the Church's 'surveillance of a sleepless eye' (*V.* 409), Lucy finds 'the assurance of his sleepless interest which broke on me like a light from heaven' (*V.* 487). During his absence, in marked contrast to the 'stone' and 'scorpion' which Caroline Helstone must digest in *Shirley* (*S.* 89–90), M. Paul gives Lucy 'neither a stone, nor an excuse – neither a scorpion, nor a disappointment; his letters were real food that nourished, living water that refreshed' (*V.* 494).

This emotional surety coexists, however, with narrative uncertainty. The parting which Lucy expects to 'harrow' her passes quietly; the years of M. Paul's absence are 'the three happiest years of my life' (*V.* 493), and the seven-day storm which leaves the Atlantic 'strewn with wrecks' (*V.* 495) as M. Paul returns becomes the occasion for Lucy's final evasion: 'Here pause: pause at once. There is enough said. Trouble no quiet, kind heart; leave sunny imaginations hope. Let it be theirs to conceive the delight of joy born again fresh out of great terror, the rapture of rescue from peril, the wondrous reprieve from dread, the fruition of return. Let them picture union and a happy succeeding life' (*V.* 496). The ambiguous ending is supposed to have been written to please Patrick Brontë , who did not want a tragic outcome (G. 414), but it is hard not to believe that Charlotte is here manipulating her narrative to give to her heroine two rewards which she feared were in reality incompatible – her independence and the assurance that for her chosen companion, she is the 'dearest, first on earth' (*V.* 491).

6

Readers and Reproducers

It All Began with Jane Eyre[1]

It was *Jane Eyre*, among Charlotte Brontë's works, which made
the greatest and most lasting impact. The obvious reason for this
is its immediate engagement with its readers, its appeal for
sympathy with its victimized heroine. Strangely, however, it is
also the novel's ideological ambiguity which continues to
challenge and intrigue readers – is it revolutionary or conservative? feminist or conformist? This uncertainty has meant
that readers can find in the novel what they want to find, while
those who reproduce it for stage or film, or extend it in fictional
prequel, parallel or sequel can, by shifting the emphasis ever so
little, present a version of the story tipped one way or another,
to suit changing times and changing preoccupations.

This book appears in a series entitled 'Writers and their
Work', and has thus tried to place Charlotte Brontë's writing in
the context of her life, but the subsequent history of her work
and the ways in which it has been interpreted show that its
significance cannot be limited to her own lifetime. Following the
changing interpretations of her work from the time of
publication to the present day produces something like an
ideological history of those times, and this chapter will follow
some of the twists and turns in this history, linking popular
adaptations to academic studies and literary reappraisals.

Jane Eyre's situation as an orphan, finding security only after
an early life isolated and exploited by those who should protect
her, closely conforms to a dominant structure of early-nine-
teenth-century popular culture. Like Dickens's child heroes –
Oliver Twist, David Copperfield, Little Nell – Jane Eyre could
easily figure as a heroine of melodrama. Peter Brooks, in his

book, *The Melodramatic Imagination* (1976), argues that Victorian stage melodrama had its origins in the revolutionary protests of the French Revolution, yet had evolved in such a way as to make its protest largely unthreatening.[2] Typically a melodrama would raise great sympathy for an oppressed individual, especially a girl child, only to remove all difficulties by a purely individual solution such as marriage or inheritance. In this way theatre-goers, who included the working class, could indulge their feelings of outrage against class enemies such as cruel employers, aristocratic landlords or would-be rapists, while having their anger soothed again not by a restructuring of society but by purely poetic justice.

This similarity in outline of course omits the complex originality of Charlotte Brontë's novel, but it helps to explain why it was so eagerly assimilated into the melodramatic tradition. In January, 1848, only three months after the novel's publication, John Courtney's play, *Jane Eyre: or, The Secrets of Thornfield Manor*, was on stage at London's notoriously working-class Victoria Theatre.[3] Building on the Victoria's reputation for plays about working-class heroines, Courtney emphasizes Jane's subordinate class status and at Lowood school he aligns her with an invented cast of comic but rebellious servants. Neither Jane nor the servants suffer in silence and Jane declares her grievances aloud in dramatic soliloquies, but the servants are entirely appeased by more humane employment at Thornfield Hall, and Jane marries Rochester just as Cinderella gets her Prince, without any of Charlotte Brontë's wary negotiation about women's status within marriage. The play thus alters the emphasis of the novel in two, almost opposite, ways. On the one hand, it increases the emphasis on Jane's victim status, but, on the other hand, it is satisfied with a purely conventional happy ending.

In Courtney's play, the focus is shifted towards the servants to such an extent that Rochester's genteel friends remain off-stage. A year later, however, John Brougham's New York version of *Jane Eyre* brought them into prominence so that Jane may triumph over them. In the novel, Jane suffers by listening in silence to the Ingrams' mocking of governesses, but in Brougham's play, she answers back, declaring that 'the mind that's conscious of its own superiority stands on too high an eminence to be reached by the petty shafts of pride and ignorance'.[4] Lord Ingram recognizes that he has been 'snubbed, by Jove!', and the scene ends with *'Tableaux of astonishment'*.[5] This play is, if anything, even readier to resolve all difficulties in the direction of the status quo, and ends with the marriage of Jane and Rochester applauded by a chorus of peasants cheering Rochester as a good landlord and 'The Farmer's Friend'.[6]

By 1870, the German playwright Charlotte Birch-Pfeiffer gave another emphasis to Charlotte Brontë's novel in her play, *Die Waise von Lowood* (*The Orphan of Lowood*), which was itself adapted, translated and repeatedly performed all over Europe (including England) until at least the end of the century. Like the British melodramatists, Birch-Pfeiffer emphasized the victim status of her heroine together with her integrity, independence and spirit, aiming, as in her other plays, to create a role model for self-reliant young women. Instead of having Jane wrestle with moral decisions, however, she simply shows her as choosing an unambiguously righteous partner. Thus her Rochester is not only elevated to the peerage as 'Lord Rowland Rochester', but is also transformed into a paragon of altruism. This madwoman, it emerges after some suspense, is actually the wife of Rochester's dead brother, whom he has taken in out of the goodness of his heart, together with Adèle, her illegitimate daughter.[7]

By contrast, James Willing's 1879 play, *Jane Eyre: or, Poor Relations*, emphasizes Rochester's culpability by creating a parallel plot in which a grown-up John Reed seduces Blanche Ingram by performing a mock marriage. After Jane has fled from Rochester's own attempt at a false marriage, and is established in her modest school-house, Blanche appears on her doorstep abandoned and begging for water. In the manner of melodrama, she declares her wrongs: as a 'cast off mistress' she will bear the whole of society's blame, while the man who has betrayed her is free to 'send more innocent souls to perdition'.[8] In this play, Jane's escape from Thornfield is explicitly motivated by her desire to preserve her 'honour', but Blanche's fate vividly underlines the fact that 'honour' is not just an abstract and personal quality, but that its loss carries severe social penalties.

The implied criticism of Rochester in Willing's play becomes marked in W. G. Wills's 1882 version, in which the action is restricted to Thornfield, and Jane is rescued from Rochester's

81

attempted bigamy by all the women in the house (Mrs Fairfax, Grace Poole, Blanche Ingram and her mother), who one by one warn her to leave at once, either because of Rochester's profligate past, or, finally, because of his previous marriage. Jane's reaction in this play is strikingly different from that of Charlotte Brontë's heroine, who confides to the reader that she 'forgave him at the moment, and on the spot' when she first sees him after the failed wedding (*JE* 298). In Wills's play, she is bitter:

> what have I to say! but that I have been a poor truthful vain fool, and you have purposed to destroy me, without pity or warning. What have I to say, but that you spread your net well, and I could detect [no] false ring in all your kindness. Oh! Sir, in whom am I to believe, when the one I could have worshipped has proved an enemy? ... You have done me a bitter wrong, that will follow me through life. Henceforth I'll distrust everything I love, I'll think everything happy must be hollow.[9]

The contrast between the ultra-virtuous Rochester of Birch-Pfeiffer's play, and this deeply culpable figure can, perhaps, be explained by the social context of Wills's play. 1882, the year of its performance, saw the culmination of what was called 'The Women's Revolt' – the lengthy and highly-publicized feminist campaign for the repeal of the Contagious Diseases Acts, which allowed any woman suspected of being a prostitute to be forcibly examined by the police. The campaign, led by Josephine Butler, turned public disapproval away from the 'fallen woman' and towards the men who had hitherto preyed on women with impunity.

The striking differences between these Victorian plays show that Charlotte Brontë's novel was open to almost opposite interpretations of Rochester's character, but they all remain within the melodramatic convention which placed the wronged heroine on a pedestal where, in Brooks's words, 'her demonstration, her representation, of virtue strikes with almost physical force, astounding and convincing'.[10]

For many of Charlotte's first women readers, however, it was not so much Jane's virtue as her courage and her spirit which they found inspiring, and a number of female novelists seemed to take courage from her example. In the aftermath of *Jane Eyre*, Julia Kavanagh, Dinah Mulock Craik and Elizabeth Gaskell produced novels in which the heroine suffers from the constraints of conventional femininity and yearns, not for love and marriage but for satisfying work which would provide dignity and independence for the single woman. In Kavanagh's *Nathalie* (1850), Craik's *Olive* (1850) and Gaskell's *North and South* (1854-5), when the heroines do encounter love, they are, like Jane Eyre, wary of the subordination which marriage entailed in Victorian England.[11]

The novelist Margaret Oliphant, in a review of 'Modern Novels' written in 1855, cites *Jane Eyre* as the origin of this marked change in novelistic conventions. Recalling an earlier period, when 'our lovers were humble and devoted' and 'our ladies were beautiful', she writes that

> suddenly there stole upon the scene, without either flourish of trumpets or public proclamation, a little fierce incendiary, doomed to turn the world of fancy upside down ... – a dangerous little person, inimical to the peace of society ... [an] impetuous little spirit which dashed into our well-ordered world, broke its boundaries, and defied its principles – and the most alarming revolution of modern time has followed the invasion of *Jane Eyre*.[12]

What Oliphant sees in Charlotte's novel and its imitators, is nothing less than 'a wild declaration of the "Rights of Woman" in a new aspect'. Here, she writes, is something more dangerous than the French Revolution. After all, 'France is but one of the Western Powers; woman is the half of the world'.[13]

By 1867, Oliphant was noting a further 'singular change' which 'has passed upon our light literature' – the phenomenon known as 'the sensation novel'. Oliphant complains that in novels such as Ellen Wood's *East Lynne* (1861), Mary Elizabeth Braddon's *Lady Audley's Secret* (1862) and Rhoda Broughton's *Cometh up as a Flower* (1867), the heroines write shamelessly about the physical demonstrations of love, and she is explicit that 'the change perhaps began at the same time when Jane Eyre made what advanced critics call her "protest" against the conventionalities in which the world clothes itself'.[14]

> What is held up to us as the story of the feminine soul as it really exists underneath its conventional coverings, is a very fleshly and unlovely record. Women driven wild with love for the man who leads them on to desperation before he accords that word of

encouragement which carries them into the seventh heaven; ... women, at the very least of it, who give and receive burning kisses and frantic embraces, and live in a voluptuous dream, either waiting for or brooding over the inevitable lover, – such are the heroines who have been imported into modern fiction.[15]

Oliphant is, of course, influenced by her Victorian expectations of gender relations, but the modern critic Winifred Hughes confirms that it was *Jane Eyre* which helped liberate the sensational imagination: in its wake, she writes, we find ' an inordinate proliferation of domestic secrets and maniacs under lock and key. But in the authentic sensation novel Jane no longer runs away from the would-be bigamist; she is much more likely to dabble in a little bigamy of her own'.[16]

Charlotte herself drew the line at bigamy, but she did have an ideal of passionate love. In *Jane Eyre*, Jane responds to Rochester with 'veins running fire' (*JE* 317), and she knows that to 'endure all the forms of love' from St John Rivers would be 'a martyrdom' (*JE* 405). Charlotte herself refused five proposals of marriage from men she felt unable to love with passion, and in *Villette* Lucy seems to resign herself to a life without such love. It is touching to know, therefore, that as soon as *Villette* was dispatched to the publishers, Charlotte received a proposal from the sober, apparently stolid Arthur Bell Nicholls, her father's curate, whose long-suppressed emotion finally revealed itself as genuine passion. 'The spectacle of one ordinarily so statue-like – thus trembling, stirred, and overcome gave me a kind of strange shock', she wrote (*L.* iii. 93). When Nicholls was on the point of leaving Haworth, driven away by Patrick's fierce hostility to the marriage, Charlotte discovered him 'in a paroxysm of anguish – sobbing as women never sob' (*L.* iii. 168). Gradually she wore down her father's antagonism, and they were married in June 1854. Surprises followed: Nicholls's relations proved to be highly respectable Irish landowners, and, more important, Charlotte liked being married. Less than a year later, however, she died, in the early stages of pregnancy. Shortly before her death, she asked her husband, 'I am not going to die, am I? ... we have been so happy' (G. 455).

Her brief married life was a busy one as she engaged with the social duties of a curate's wife with novel enthusiasm, and one question which must have presented itself to her was how she was to continue with her writing. The only fiction which we know to have been written during this time is the fragment called *Emma*, which opens a story about a girl abandoned in a girls' boarding school.[17] During her last visit to London, in January 1853, Charlotte had asked to be shown, instead of places of entertainment, a number of utilitarian institutions, including Newgate and Pentonville (two notorious prisons), the Foundling Hospital for orphans and the Bethlehem or Bedlam Hospital for the insane (B. 842). In writing to George Smith about *Villette*, she had lamented that 'I cannot write books handling the topics of the day' (L. iii. 75), and it may be that she was trying to acquire knowledge that would fit her to write a 'social problem' novel. The modern novelist Clare Boylan has exploited this possibility in her continuation of Charlotte's *Emma*. Boylan's *Emma Brown* (2003) is improbably sensational with its sordid low-life scenes, but it opens the intriguing speculation that if Charlotte had lived, she might have ventured into more challenging social situations.[18]

After Charlotte's death, Patrick asked her friend, the eminent novelist Elizabeth Gaskell, to write a memoir of his daughter, and Gaskell went about her task with characteristic vigour. Not only did she travel extensively in order to interview people who had known Charlotte, but she had access to the hundreds of letters which Charlotte had written to her friend Ellen Nussey. Gaskell's *Life of Charlotte Brontë* (1857) thus included a great deal more personal detail than was usual for biographies of public figures, and Gaskell had a particular reason for this.[19] Although Charlotte's work had been well received on the whole, there was a persistent perception among readers and critics that her work was 'coarse' – a word which conveys very little to modern readers. What they objected to was Charlotte's freedom in speaking particularly of the physical aspects of love. Rochester's confessions of extra-marital affairs to the young, unmarried Jane, for instance, were seen as quite improper.

One of Gaskell's aims, therefore, was to present her friend to the world as an impeccably respectable and virtuous woman; she wrote to George Smith that she wanted to 'make the world ...honour the woman as much as they have admired the writer'.[20] Her method was to emphasize Charlotte's hard life and self-sacrificing nature, her harsh physical environment, her multiple bereavements, her troublesome brother and her devotion to a father whom Gaskell presented as eccentric and autocratic. The *Life* was eagerly read, and as Miriam Allott remarks, among the more educated reviewers, this 'better understanding' of Charlotte's life 'disposed of the narrower moral issues in the old controversy about the Brontës' "coarseness" and "immorality"'.[21] When Matthew Arnold, by then Professor of Poetry at Oxford University, wrote his influential essay, 'The Function of Criticism at the Present Time' (1864), he was happy to include Charlotte Brontë in what he called the 'canon', or body of acknowledged 'great' literature.

This more decorous reputation did not, however, recommend Charlotte's work to every reader. In the 1850s and 1860s, young women were riveted by Jane Eyre's bold declaration of independence, but as the nineteenth century drew on, feminist readers became critical of the outcome of the novel. As the Victorian women's movement, or 'first-wave feminism', got under way with its demands for the vote, improved education and access to the professions, Jane Eyre's happy marriage, for those involved in these campaigns, came to seem a retrograde step. This is just one way in which Charlotte Brontë's work provokes almost opposite responses. Women who share Jane's particular sense of oppression will find her protest a powerful statement of women's rights and will feel that a companionate marriage based on financial and intellectual equality is a goal worth striving for. Women whose horizons have broadened to include higher education and professional work may well find Jane's utopia merely a new prison.

By the early twentieth century, *Jane Eyre* was widely regarded as a 'safe' classic with a conventional courtship-and-marriage plot, and this perception was reinforced by the writings of Sigmund Freud. In his *Three Essays on the Theory of Sexuality* (1905) and his later essays on 'Female Sexuality' (1931) and 'Femininity' (1933), Freud outlines the development of what he saw as 'normal' femininity by way of the 'Oedipus complex': a little girl who is at first attached, like all babies, to her mother, comes to recognize the social inferiority of women and, perceiving that she cannot on the other hand *be* a man, seeks instead to displace her mother and attach herself to her father. When this proves impossible, she aims instead to marry a father-like man.

The feminist novelist and critic May Sinclair, who was herself professionally involved in promulgating Freud's psychoanalytic methods, made two almost contradictory responses to the Brontës in the light of Freud's theories. In her biography, *The Three Brontës* (1912), she briskly disposes of the Victorian view of Charlotte as a 'lachrymose, middle-aged spinster... for ever whining over the frustration of her sex', presenting the sisters as articulate heroines, saved from conventional femininity by a fortunate upbringing and clear intellect.[22] In her novel, *The Three Sisters* (1914), however, although the three sisters of the title bear obvious similarities to the Brontës (being daughters of a north-country parson, for instance), she gives full weight to Freud's pessimistic account of the difficulties, for women, of surmounting the Oedipus complex, presenting the sisters as text-book examples of Freud's three possibilities for female development: normal femininity, masculinity complex and hysteria.[23]

Freud, of course, derived his theories from his observation of conventional Victorian families, and while Sinclair, in her biography, wanted to rescue the Brontë sisters from that depressing pattern, her novel suggests that his analysis matched a wider social reality. Here, in fact, is another reason for the persistent popularity of *Jane Eyre*. Its story of a young, powerless woman who seeks the affection of an older, richer man in the face of a hostile other woman, exactly replicates what Freud saw as the pattern of normal femininity, and it is surely this apparent social orthodoxy which made *Jane Eyre* a favourite for early film adaptation; at least thirteen silent film versions were produced before the first 'talkie' in 1934. Technical contraints meant that these silent films were short and called for drastic cutting, and as Patricia Ingham concludes, 'these omissions from the story as related in the novel deliver a conventional love story, untrammelled by the examination of moral issues and with a single-minded heroine who knows right from wrong and is not tempted by sin'.[24]

Virginia Woolf, writing in 1928, saw clearly that Charlotte Brontë's position was conflicted. 'The writer was meeting criticism', she writes, 'she was saying this by way of aggression, or that by way of conciliation. She was admitting that she was "only a woman" or protesting that she was "as good as a man"'.[25] The film-makers, however, adopted only the traditional half of this dialogue, and *Jane Eyre*'s absorption into mainstream culture reaches its culmination in the 1943 film version directed by Robert Stevenson, in which Orson Welles plays Mr Rochester. Joan Fontaine, as Jane, is completely cowed in this version by Welles's loud and overbearingly masculine interpretation of his role, and his performance is supported by both the writing and the direction of the film. This Rochester never appears vulnerable, from the beginning, where he does not need Jane's help after falling from his horse, to the final scenes, where his injuries are much milder than in the novel. Jane, meanwhile, loses much of her spoken defiance. Instead of the verbal sparring which, in the novel, enlivens their first interview at Thornfield Hall, she submissively stoops to bathe his injured foot.

From the 1930s onwards, the 'triangular' *Jane Eyre* plot – young, vulnerable heroine, masterful older man, hostile 'other' woman – quickly became the basis of the 'formula' romances developed by Mills & Boon and, given its uncanny similarity to Freud's 'normal' femininity, we might accept it as inevitable.[26] In *The Female Eunuch* (1970), however, Germaine Greer challenges women to take responsibility for their submission to this dominating hero. 'This', she writes, 'is the hero that women have chosen for themselves. The traits invented for him have been invented by women cherishing the chains of their bondage'.[27] The Mills & Boon plot has evolved in response to social change, so that where 1950s romances ended with a kiss and a promise of marriage, those of the twenty-first century are likely to include explicit pre-marital sex and a satisfying post-marital career for both partners. Nevertheless the basic structure of the plot is remarkably durable.

Already during the interwar period, however, more independent women writers, signalling their intention by explicit allusion, chose to re-write the *Jane Eyre* plot in ways which suggested that conventional marriage was not a good outcome for modern women. Elizabeth von Arnim's *Vera* (1921) is a macabre Gothic version in which a vulnerable orphan marries an older man in return for security, only to discover that he has effectively killed his first wife by a regime of subtle domestic tyranny. Like Daphne du Maurier's *Rebecca* (1938), *Vera* takes its title not from the Jane Eyre character but from the first wife, and both novels play on the Bluebeard parallel which is briefly alluded to in *Jane Eyre* itself (*JE* 107). Tania Modleski, in her book, *Loving with a Vengeance* (1982), points out that the unequal power relationship between men and women within conventional marriage can, for the woman, easily tip from romance to paranoia.[28] *Vera* is the more chilling in that its heroine does not escape; despite warnings from an older relative, she continues to 'cherish the chains of her bondage'. Twenty-five years later, Elizabeth Taylor's *Palladian* (1946) is a self-consciously literary pastiche in which *Wuthering Heights* undercuts the *Jane Eyre* model in a kind of black comedy. Its sprightly governess heroine marries her employer, but as they re-enter his crumbling mansion its shadow seems to darken their future.

It is interesting to compare Daphne du Maurier's *Rebecca* (1938) with Winifred Holtby's almost contemporary *South Riding* (1936). Both use *Jane Eyre*'s 'triangular plot', in which a taciturn hero with a landed estate and a disastrous first marriage encounters a new young woman. Both, like *Jane Eyre* itself, end with the destruction of the great house, as if to say goodbye to the upper-class Victorian way of life, but their conclusions are critical of the *Jane Eyre* pattern in different ways. The young heroine in *Rebecca* marries the Rochester figure and ends up complicit with him in disposing of his first wife, but the memory of Rebecca and of the great house haunt them, effectively trapping them in the past. Like *Vera*, *Rebecca* has some of the atmosphere of a ghost story, which derives, in these novels about second wives, from 'the uncanny sensation that the past is repeating itself'.[29] The implication is that marriage itself requires women to see their individual identity subsumed in a social role, in an uncanny repetition of previous lives which induces paranoia.

While the heroines of *Vera* and *Rebecca* are very young and vulnerable, Sarah Burton, in *South Riding*, is already an independent, well educated, well travelled woman at the outset of the novel, when she is appointed headmistress of a girls' school. Her story is embedded in a complex social panorama linked by the operations of local government in education, health, transport and social welfare, and her relationship with Robert Carne, the Rochester figure, is emblematic of the collision between her new and vigorous concept of a democratic and cooperative world with his land-based and conservative values based on class distinction and his honourable but out-dated shouldering of the responsibility entailed by privilege. Sarah's passionate and irrational love for Carne, defying all sensible constraints, would have led her to abandon everything she has worked for – her career and independence – had he not died before she can commit herself to him. Despite her desperate grief the novel ends positively with her plans for the school. Although Holtby allows her heroine's future to be determined by a stroke of chance, the novel does not evade the debate on the ongoing problem, for women, of balancing love and independence.

Although these interwar novels all present critical perspectives on *Jane Eyre*, they appealed to the same kind of audience as the Victorian novel, an audience which took the story as an extension of real life, and judged it by whether they liked or disliked the characters and approved or disapproved of what they did. During the early years of the twentieth century, however, the Modernist movement introduced the idea that a novel could be judged like a picture or a piece of music, by its form as well as by its morality. Sophisticated readers began to value features such as structures of parallels and contrasts, and *Jane Eyre* became interesting again as they noticed that the obnoxious Reed cousins, for instance, a boy and two girls, are balanced by the exemplary Rivers cousins, a man and two women. The repulsive evangelical Mr Brocklehurst is contrasted with the charismatic evangelical St John Rivers. St John, cold and ambitious, is contrasted with Rochester, passionate and impulsive. Jane's experience throughout the novel is shaped by contrasts between red and white, fire and ice, summer and winter, starvation and plenty, imprisonment and escape.

Some formalistic readings of this kind existed separately from social meanings, but the recognition of literary patterns was partly prompted not only by psychoanalysis, which offered symbolic interpretation of dreams, events and images, but by the new science of social anthropology, which saw structures of opposition as basic to social hierarchies. When second-wave feminism began in the late 1960s, therefore, the formal structures of *Jane Eyre* took on social meanings relating to women's lot. The relationship between Jane and Bertha, in particular, began to gain prominence. Victorian stage versions of *Jane Eyre* list Bertha simply as 'the maniac', exploiting her noisy violence, and her vivid contrast with Jane, for sensational effect, and this treatment persists as late as 1936 in Helen Jerome's stage play, which is still performed by amateur groups.

Many twentieth-century versions, in the aftermath of Freud, emphasized the link between Bertha's madness and her uninhibited sexuality, since a 'normal' female would have repressed these impulses. Elaine Showalter's 1977 feminist classic, *A Literature of their Own*, represents Bertha as 'the incarnation of the flesh, of female sexuality in its most irredeemably bestial and terrifying form'. For Showalter, Jane can only 'become truly her "own mistress"' by 'destroying the dark passion of her own psyche'.[30] The 1986 stage version by Fay Weldon and Helena Kaut-Howson was in this tradition, representing the Lowood girls, and sometimes Jane and Charlotte, as life-sized dolls dressed in grey, emphasizing the lifeless dreariness of Victorian women's lives, while in contrast, Bertha in a swirling red dress suggested uncontrolled desire.[31]

Sandra Gilbert and Susan Gubar's book, *The Madwoman in the Attic* (1979), while sharing many of these assumptions, shifts the emphasis by positing an unlikely parallel between the apparently contrasted characters, Jane and Bertha. Reading the novel as 'a story of enclosure and escape', they argue that both Jane and Bertha know what it is like to be locked up, and to have passion threaten sanity as it does when Rochester tempts Jane to become his mistress (*JE* 317).[32] Gilbert and Gubar's reading of *Jane Eyre* has clearly become a new orthodoxy. In 1998, Polly Teale's West End stage success made visible the parallel between Jane and Bertha by having a dancer, also in a red dress, accompany all Jane's actions, representing by her wild movements the 'hunger, rebellion and rage' which Jane cannot articulate within the conventions of her time.[33] In 2000, the composer Michael Berkeley produced an opera based on *Jane Eyre*, with a libretto by David Malouf, in which, again, the figure of the madwoman is present throughout (again dressed in red), often sharing Jane's music.[34] In particular they both sing and dance to a theme from Donizetti's opera *Lucia di Lammermoor* – an inspired choice since not only was Charlotte Brontë a devoted reader of Sir Walter Scott, whose *Bride of Lammermoor* provides Donizetti's story, but Lucia (or Lucy), the 'bride' of the title, goes mad and kills her husband after an enforced marriage.

More than ten years before *The Madwoman in the Attic*, Jean Rhys had given us a Lucia-like perspective on the madwoman in her beautiful and moving novel, *Wide Sargasso Sea* (1966).[35] Rhys's novel is not interested in parallels between Jane and Bertha, but allows Bertha to tell her own story. Thus we learn that Bertha is the name which Rochester gave to his girl-bride, Antoinette, when their marriage was arranged by the older male members of both families. Antoinette, educated in a convent, knows nothing of sex until Rochester initiates her, but then, disgusted by the sexual freedoms he himself has encouraged, he defines her as mad and confines her at Thornfield. The red dress which appears in so many adaptations derives from Rhys's novel, where it is the only thing to remind Antoinette, in cold, grey England, of her tropical Caribbean homeland. In this novel it is Jane Eyre who makes fleeting and unsympathetic appearances, and its narrative thus acts in the way that Elaine Showalter describes as characteristic of the best feminist criticism, which 'present[s us] with a radical alteration of our vision, a demand that we see meaning in what has hitherto been empty space. The orthodox plot recedes, and another plot, hitherto submerged in the anonymity of the background, stands out in bold relief like a thumbprint'.[36] *Wide Sargasso Sea* had an almost immediate impact on visual conceptions of 'the madwoman'. In Delbert Mann's 1970 film, Bertha appears not as the Victorian 'maniac' but as a young, wistful woman, as she does in Franco Zeffirelli's film of 1996.

Wide Sargasso Sea is an exquisitely written novel which does not depend on its relation to *Jane Eyre* for its power to engage its readers, but when read as a 'prequel', it also achieves something rare among 'derivative' writing: it creates a new and striking work, while at the same time enhancing our understanding of its pre-text. Rhys's representation of context and motive deepens our response not only to Antoinette/Bertha, but even to Rochester (recognizable though unnamed in this novel). Although Rhys seems uninterested in Jane Eyre, other writers have been intrigued by the possibility of relating the two novels. Debbie Shewell's play, *More than one Antoinette* (1990), for the Monstrous Regiment theatre company, had already explored this relationship when Polly Teale addressed the topic in *After Mrs Rochester* (2003).[37] This play includes the troubled Jean Rhys herself in the complex of parallels between Jane and Antoinette, and used as stage properties large reproductions of the illustrations to *Jane Eyre* by the Portuguese-born artist Paula Rego, which were independently exhibited in 2002.[38] Rego, who used the same model for Jane and Bertha, tells us that she 'came to Jane Eyre' from '*Wide Sargasso Sea*', confirming the complicated reciprocal influences now established between these two texts.[39] Her Rochester, like the men in many of her pictures, is a ruthless-looking, jack-booted figure, and in 'Come to Me', where Jane hears Rochester's call, she appears in the grip of a fierce but indecisive desire: 'I put her doubting', Rego comments.[40]

By contrast with these stage plays, which dramatize Jane's inner conflicts, some film and television versions from the 1970s onwards have tried to rehabilitate her as a feminist heroine. In Delbert Mann's 1970 film, for instance, Susannah York and George C. Scott soberly discuss their situation in relation to his existing marriage. Television here has the advantage of space, and the 1983 BBC television version produced by Julian Amyes was able to devote eleven episodes to the slow unfolding of the relationship between Jane and Rochester. Zelah Clarke and Timothy Dalton in this version created a truly absorbing representation of the story, and viewers who were thus able to appreciate Jane's control of the situation, whether through repartee or through inspired eloquence, received a very different impression from those who saw only a truncated version of the plot.

The demands of big-budget, internationally distributed films seem, however, to exert pressure towards a more conventional interpretation. Zeffirelli's 1996 film vividly enhances the scenes of Jane's childish rebellion against Aunt Reed and at Lowood School, where she stands in solidarity with Helen Burns as Brocklehurst cuts their hair. The figure of Rochester, however, though well played by William Hurt, is socially magnified, rather in the Orson Welles manner, by using Haddon Hall – an ancient and massive Derbyshire castle – in place of the 'gentleman's manor-house' described in the novel. Jane, played by Charlotte Gainsbourg, has to suffer no humiliating or dangerous exposure after leaving Thornfield, as she flees directly to known and sympathetic relatives, and the management of camera-shots suggests that as Rochester's wife she will sink into a protected femininity. These tendencies are exaggerated in Robert Young's television version for LWT (1997), where Samantha Morton is a convincing Jane but her voice-over sets the scene for a formula romance. Ciàran Hinds plays Rochester as a blustering bully and Kay Mellor's screen-play includes sensationally Gothic sequences.

More recent adaptations return to more inward themes. The 2006 BBC version, directed by Susanna White, develops the idea of an intellectual relationship between Jane and Rochester by showing him (played by Toby Stephens) as an amateur botanist and entomologist, interests in which Jane can join. Ruth Wilson delivers Jane's more outspoken speeches with passion, but her early life is dealt with in a perfunctory flash-back which emphasizes the centrality of love in her life. Cary Fukunaga's 2011 film is the only recent version to rival the 1983 television adaptation. Although necessarily shorter, the film achieves dramatic tension by beginning with Jane's escape to Moor House and revealing her previous life in a series of flashbacks – a device also used in Berkeley's opera. Fukunaga minimizes the sensational elements of the plot and the dialogue closely follows that of the novel, enabling Mia Wasikowska and Michael Fassbender to give a riveting impression of the growing attraction, intellectual as well as physical, between Jane and Rochester.

These stage and visual representations of *Jane Eyre* do not on the whole interfere with the outcome of Charlotte Brontë's plot. Recent fictional sequels, however, take a variety of stances on Jane's future life. Hilary Bailey's *Mrs Rochester* (1997) and Kimberley A. Bennet's coyly sexual *Jane Rochester* (2000) manufacture enough potential problems to keep the story going, but restore good relations between Jane and Rochester in the end. D. M. Thomas's *Charlotte: the Final Journey of Jane Eyre* (2000)[41] is a much more complicated affair, with several narrative voices and time schemes which interact with one another. It begins with what seems to be a continuation of Jane's autobiography, in which Jane escapes from an unconsummated marriage with Rochester to seek his son (by Bertha) in Martinique. The narrative then shifts to a present-day academic who at first claims to have written 'Jane's' text, but then suggests that it is genuine Charlotte Brontë. The three women are linked by markedly Oedipal relationships with their fathers or father-figures, but the overall effect of this ambitious, sexually provocative, post-modernist novel is to cast doubt on the stability of written texts. A delightfully comic version of this instability is found in Jasper Fforde's *The Eyre Affair* (2001), in which a time-travelling literary detective becomes trapped inside *Jane Eyre* and alters its ending for ever.[42] Two novels by Laura Joh Rowland (2009, 2010) offer similarly witty, thrilling and historically accurate, though implausible, adventures for Charlotte Brontë herself, involving the same low-life scenes as *Emma Brown* together with historical figures including Queen Victoria.[43]

Novelists have also exploited the possibilities of exploring minor characters in the novel, such as Robbie Kydd's *The Quiet Stranger* (1991), which invents a pre-history for Bertha Mason's brother, Richard.[44] Of two versions of a biography for Adèle Varens, Emma Tennant's *The French Dancer's Bastard* (2002) is a sensational story involving much confusion about the dates and details of the narrative, and many implausible inventions including an aristocratic twin brother for Adèle.[45] Claire Moïse's *Adèle, Grace and Céline: the Other Women of Jane Eyre* (2009), on the other hand, is a thoughtful book in which Adèle, having attended the 'first blue-stocking girls' school in England' and Bedford College, goes to the Crimea with Florence Nightingale.[46]

The seemingly unlimited possibilities for deriving new stories from the *Jane Eyre* original are demonstrated by two recent novels, one of which – Melanie M. Jeschke's *Jillian Dare* (2009) – presents the present-day Jane figure as an earnest and unrebellious Christian, and the other – Sherri Browning Erwin's *Jane Slayre* (2010) – reinvents the plot as a vampire novel.[47] A dispiriting development is the fiction which alludes to *Jane Eyre* simply as a launching pad for essentially unrelated invention. Margot Livesey's *The Flight of Gemma Hardy* (2012), for instance, though marketed as 'a captivating homage to Charlotte Brontë's *Jane Eyre*', is a lively and interesting modern story which in fact gains nothing from its clumsy and intermittent pinning to the *Jane Eyre* plot.[48]

Like the fiction of the interwar period, some present-day

fiction makes a comment on the validity of the *Jane Eyre* plot for contemporary readers. There are stories addressed to teenage readers, such as Sheila Greenwald's *It All Began with Jane Eyre* (1980), or Kay Woodward's more recent *Jane Airhead* (2009), which warn against making *Jane Eyre* an exact template for their lives,[49] and stories which weave a consciousness of the earlier story into present-day experience, such as Jennifer Vandever's *The Brontë Project* (2005).[50] There are also fleeting allusions in coming-of-age fiction as varied as Maya Angelou's *I Know Why the Caged Bird Sings* (1969),[51] Jeanette Winterson's *Oranges are not the only Fruit* (1985)[52] or Tsitsi Dangarembga's *Nervous Conditions* (1988).[53]

None of Charlotte Brontë's other works have attracted the same attention as *Jane Eyre*, although *Shirley* was filmed, on location in and near Haworth, as early as 1922. *Villette* was dramatized for television in 1957 and 1970, and in 1997 Judith Adams adapted the novel in a stage version which recreated its Victorian context by quotations from Christina Rossetti and Emily Dickinson. The novel presents a challenge to adaptors because of the intensely inward nature of its movement, but in 2005 the adaptor Lisa Evans in collaboration with the Frantic Assembly theatre company developed an innovative solution to this problem in a version of *Villette* combining key speeches from the novel with choreographed movement which vividly rendered the story's inner emotion.[54]

It is *Jane Eyre* which remains Charlotte Brontë's enduring legacy to the general culture. As well as specific adaptations and fictional reworkings of the novel, literature is full of incidental references which attest to its powerful influence thoughout the world. Its persistent appeal surely lies in its ability to keep us puzzled. *Jane Eyre* is a great novel not because it gives us clear answers, but because its complex story dramatizes women's contradictory desires, for freedom and for security, for status and for solidarity with the oppressed.

Charlotte Brontë's appeal is not, however, limited to *Jane Eyre*. Heather Glen's edition of the later juvenilia invites a new and fascinated response to these unexpectedly jaunty, ironic, socially 'knowing' texts. *Shirley* yields unexpected perspectives as a critique of conventional religion. Among thoughtful readers, *Villette* continues to challenge interpretation. Although its obvious appeal is through its wrenching representation of loneliness and despair, its closely-written narrative yields meaning in surprisingly different ways. Three notable essays, for instance, have opened quite varied perspectives on the novel. Mary Jacobus's 'The Buried Letter' offers a psycho-analytic view of the novel's struggle with Romanticism; Sally Shuttleworth's 'The Surveillance of a Sleepless Eye' reads the novel in terms of institutional and ideological constraint; and Heather Glen's chapters on '*Villette* and History' place it in the context of a bewildering mid-Victorian burgeoning of material artifacts.[55] Essays such as these remind us that Charlotte Brontë is not just a romantic best-seller but a writer of considerable complexity, whose knowledge and critical appraisal of her times raise surprising resonances in our own.

Charlotte Brontë is, in fact, that rare phenomenon, a writer who can entrance children and general readers, provoking endless revisionings of her work, while offering ever-new avenues of exploration for academic scrutiny. For the new reader, she opens a world of vivid experience, while repeated readings yield layer upon layer of meaning.

Notes

CHAPTER 1. EARLY LIFE AND EARLY WRITING

1. Janet Gezari (ed.), *Emily Jane Brontë: The Complete Poems* (Harmondsworth: Penguin, 1992), 31.
2. J. A. V. Chapple and Arthur Pollard (eds), *The Letters of Mrs Gaskell* [1966] (Manchester: Manchester University Press, 1997), 124.
3. Ibid. 398.
4. Charlotte's writing between 1826 and 1839 is generally described as her 'juvenilia' or 'early writing'. Christine Alexander has published an analytical monograph, *The Early Writings of Charlotte Brontë* (Oxford: Blackwell, 1983) and also *An Edition of the Early Writings of Charlotte Brontë*, 2 vols (Oxford: Shakespeare Head Press, 1987, 1991), which, however, only covers the years 1826–35 so far. Alexander has, however, published a selection of writings from the whole period (including writing by Branwell, Emily and Anne) in *The Brontës: Tales of Glass Town, Angria, and Gondal: Selected Writings* (Oxford: Oxford World's Classics, 2010). Heather Glen's edition, *Charlotte Brontë: Tales of Angria* (Harmondsworth: Penguin, 2006) offers five of Charlotte's 'novelettes' written 1838–9.
5. In the early nineteenth century, the 'Tory' political faction supported the monarchy and landed interests, while the 'Whigs' supported the mercantile interest.
6. Letters and words in square brackets, here and elsewhere, are supplied by the editor where the manuscript is incomplete or indecipherable.
7. Juliet Barker, *The Brontës* [1994] (2nd ed., London: Abacus, 2010).
8. It was not, however, a problem which went away. As late as 1843, Patrick was writing to his brother Hugh, in Ireland, advising him and his neighbours to arm themselves so as not to be taken by surprise, but also 'admonish[ing] You, And All my Brothers, and Friends, not to be rash, and neither to break the Laws of God, or Man – And I would say, let prudence, and justice, be joined to

Courage – And due precaution'. Dudley Green (ed.), *The Letters of the Reverend Patrick Brontë* (Stroud: Nonsuch, 2005), 155. I am grateful to Sarah Fermi for this reference.

9. See Glen, *Tales of Angria*, pp. xviii–xxi.
10. Ibid. p. xv.
11. Quoted in Christine Alexander and Margaret Smith (eds), *The Oxford Companion to the Brontës* (Oxford: Oxford University Press, 2003), 113.
12. Alexander (ed.), *An Edition*, ii (1991), Part 1, p. xxi.
13. Charlotte, who was skilled at drawing, took pleasure in imagining and reproducing the beauty of these women and her portraits of Mina Laury and the Duchess of Zamorna, among others, are copied from originals in *Finden's Byron Beauties* (1836). See Christine Alexander and Jane Sellars (eds), *The Art of the Brontës* (Cambridge: Cambridge University Press, 1995).
14. Fannie Ratchford, *The Brontës' Web of Childhood* (New York: Columbia University Press, 1941), 84.
15. In Alexander (ed.), *An Edition*, ii (1991) Part 2, 92–3.
16. Glen, *Tales of Angria*, p. xix.
17. In Glen, *Tales of Angria.*
18. Ibid. 201–2.
19. Jane Austen, *Pride and Prejudice* [1813] iii. 17 (Oxford: Oxford World's Classics, 2008), 94.
20. Glen, *Tales of Angria*, p. xxiv.
21. Ibid. p. xx.
22. Anne Brontë, *Agnes Grey* [1847] (Oxford: Oxford World's Classics, 1998), 1.

CHAPTER 2. *THE PROFESSOR*

1. Elizabeth Sewell, *Principles of Education, drawn from nature and revelation, and applied to female education in the upper classes* (London, 1865), ii, 240. Quoted in M. Jeanne Peterson, 'The Victorian Governess: Status Incongruence in Family and Society', in *Suffer and Be Still: Women in the Victorian Age*, ed. Martha Vicinus (Bloomington and London: Indiana University Press, 1974) 9–10.
2. Elizabeth Rigby, unsigned review, *Quarterly Review* lxxxiv (December, 1848), 176. Quoted in Peterson, 'The Victorian Governess', 10.
3. Ibid. 176–7, quoted in ibid. 11.
4. Terry Eagleton, *Myths of Power: A Marxist Study of the Brontës* [1975] (3rd ed., Basingstoke: Palgrave Macmillan, 2005), 8.
5. Charlotte and Emily Brontë, *The Belgian Essays: A Critical Edition* ed. and trans. Sue Lonoff (New Haven and London: Yale University

Press, 1996).
6. 'A woman's "highest duty is so often to suffer and be still"': Sarah Stickney Ellis, *The Daughters of England* (London, 1845), 73.
7. *Winter Evening Thoughts: A Miscellaneous Poem* (1810), *Cottage Poems* (1811), *The Rural Minstrel: A Miscellany of Descriptive Poems* (1813), *The Cottage in the Wood* (1815), *The Maid of Killarney* (1818), *The Signs Of The Times* (1835).
8. Charlotte Brontë, 'Biographical Notice of Ellis and Acton Bell', in Emily Brontë, *Wuthering Heights*, ed. Ian Jack (Oxford: Oxford World Classics, 2009), 301.
9. Ibid. 302.
10. Ibid. 302.
11. Quoted in *Poems by the Brontë Sisters*, ed. Mark R. D. Seaward [1978] (London: A.& C. Black, 1985), p. x; also in Miriam Allott (ed.), *The Brontës: The Critical Heritage* (London: Routledge & Kegan Paul, 1974), 59–60.
12. *The Poems of Charlotte Bront*, ed. Tom Winnifrith (Oxford: Shakespeare Head Press, 1984), p. xii.
13. *Poems*, ed. Seaward, 48–9. This edition has the advantage of reproducing the selection of poems made in the original 1846 publication of *Poems by Currer, Ellis and Acton Bell* (London: Aylott & Jones). Alternatively, see *Poems*, ed. Winnifrith, 24.
14. *Poems*, ed. Seaward, 62–3, 75; *Poems*, ed. Winnifrith, 32–3, 43.
15. *Poems*, ed. Seaward, 35; *Poems*, ed. Winnifrith, 18.
16. See Elizabeth Abel et al., *The Voyage In: Fictions of Female Development* (Hanover, NH: University Press of New England, 1983); Eagleton, *Myths of Power*, 8.
17. Heather Glen, *Charlotte Brontë: The Imagination in History* [2002] (Oxford: Oxford University Press, 2004), 35; see also Heather Glen, 'Introduction', in Charlotte Brontë, *The Professor* [1857] (Harmondsworth: Penguin, 1989).
18. Glen, *Charlotte Brontë*, 47.
19. The story of how the Earl of Northangerland refuses to acknowledge his sons was begun by Branwell and taken up by Charlotte, for instance in 'The Duke of Zamorna' (Glen, *Tales of Angria*, 181) and 'Ashworth', 'The Moores' and 'Willie Ellin', in *Charlotte Brontë: Unfinished Novels*, ed. Tom Winnifrith (Stroud: Alan Sutton, 1993).
20. See Rachel Blau du Plessis, *Writing Beyond the Ending: Narrative Strategies of Twentieth-Century Women Writers* (Bloomington: Indiana University Press, 1985).
21. See Anne's *Agnes Grey* (1847) and *The Tenant of Wildfell Hall* (1848), especially ch. 3, 'A Controversy'.
22. This argument is supported at length in Glen, *Charlotte Brontë*, ch. 2.

CHAPTER 3. *JANE EYRE*

1. E[dwin] P[ercy] Whipple], 'Novels of the Season', *North American Review*, cxli (October 1848), 354–69; in Miriam Allott (ed.), *The Brontës: the Critical Heritage*, (London: Routledge & Kegan Paul, 1974), 97.
2. Quoted in Allott, *The Brontës*, 389.
3. See Patsy Stoneman, *Brontë Transformations: The Cultural Dissemination of 'Jane Eyre' and 'Wuthering Heights'* (Hemel Hempstead: Harvester Wheatsheaf/Prentice Hall, 1996); 'The Brontë Myth' in *The Cambridge Companion to the Brontës*, ed. Heather Glen (Cambridge: Cambridge University Press, 2002), relevant entries in *The Oxford Companion to the Brontës*, ed. Christine Alexander and Margaret Smith (Oxford: Oxford University Press, 2003) and 'Adaptations, Prequels, Sequels, Translations', in Marianne Thormählen (ed.), *The Brontës*, Authors in Context series (Cambridge: Cambridge University Press, 2012).
4. In Heather Glen (ed.), *Charlotte Brontë: Tales of Angria* (Harmondsworth: Penguin, 2006).
5. Not all such responses were positive: for instance Elizabeth Rigby, unsigned review, *Quarterly Review* lxxxiv (December 1848), 176 (in Allott, *The Bronts*, 109–10).
6. Terry Eagleton, *Myths of Power: A Marxist Study of the Brontës* [1975] (3rd ed., Basingstoke: Palgrave Macmillan, 2005), 8.
7. Ibid.
8. Florence Nightingale, *Cassandra* [1852], intro. Myra Stark (New York: Feminist Press, 1979), 28.
9. See Elizabeth Abel et al., *The Voyage In: Fictions of Female Development* (Hanover, NH: University Press of New England, 1983).
10. See Marianne Thormählen, *The Brontës and Religion* (Cambridge: Cambridge University Press, 1999), 21.
11. See Margot Peters, *Charlotte Brontë: Style in the Novel* (Madison: University of Wisconsin Press, 1973), ch. 5.
12. Virginia Woolf, *A Room of One's Own* [1928] (Harmondsworth: Penguin, 1970), 70.
13. Nancy Pell, 'Resistance, Rebellion, and Marriage: The Economics of *Jane Eyre*', *Nineteenth-Century Fiction* 31/4 (1977), 397–420, 419.
14. Sandra M. Gilbert and Susan Gubar, *The Madwoman in the Attic: The Woman Writer and the Nineteenth-Century Literary Imagination* (New Haven: Yale University Press, 1979).
15. Ibid. 78.
16. See Sally Shuttleworth, 'Introduction', *JE* pp. xix–xx.
17. Sigmund Freud, 'The Uncanny', in *The Pelican Freud Library* xiv, *Art and Literature* (Harmondsworth: Penguin,1985), 335–76, 364.

18. The word 'Creole' in Victorian England could mean either a white West Indian or someone of mixed race.
19. Gayatri Chakravorty Spivak, 'Three women's texts and a critique of imperialism', *Critical Inquiry* 22 (1985), 243–61.
20. Susan Meyer, 'Colonialism and the Figurative Strategy of *Jane Eyre*', in *Macropolitics of Nineteenth-Century Literature*, ed. Jonathan Arac et al. (Philadelphia: University of Pennsylvania Press, 1991), 159–83, 180. See also Susan Meyer, *Imperialism at Home: Race and Victorian Women's Fiction* (Ithaca and London: Cornell University Press, 1996), 83.
21 Spivak, 'Three Women's Texts', 245.
22 James Willing, *Jane Eyre: or, Poor Relations* (1879), in *Jane Eyre on Stage, 1848–1898: An illustrated edition of eight plays with contextual notes*, ed. Patsy Stoneman (Aldershot: Ashgate Press, 2007), 329.
23. Margaret Oliphant, 'Modern Novelists – Great and Small', *Blackwood's Magazine* lxxvii (May 1855), 557–9; in Allott, *The Brontës*, 312.

CHAPTER 4. *SHIRLEY*

1. John Courtney, *Jane Eyre: or, The Secrets of Thornfield Manor* (1848), in Patsy Stoneman (ed.), *Jane Eyre on Stage, 1848–1898: An illustrated edition of eight plays with contextual notes* (Aldershot: Ashgate Press, 2007).
2. Elizabeth Rigby, unsigned review, *Quarterly Review*, lxxxiv (Decmber 1848), 153–85; in Miriam Allott (ed.), *The Brontës: the Critical Heritage* (London: Routledge & Kegan Paul, 1974), 109–10.
3. For Patrick Brontë's enthusiasm for Wellington's Peninsular campaign, and for his personal experience of Luddite attacks in west Yorkshire, see Ch. 1, above.
4. Quoted in Heather Glen, *Charlotte Brontë: the Imagination in History* [2002] (Oxford: Oxford University Press, 2004), 157.
5. Ibid. 153–4.
6. See ibid. 147–9, for an intensive discussion of this idea, to which I am indebted.
7. Unsigned review, *Edinburgh Review*, xci (Jan. 1850), 153–73; in Allott, *The Brontës*, 165.
8. Rebecca Fraser, *Charlotte Brontë* [1988] (London: Methuen, 1989), 328.
9. Glen, *Charlotte Brontë*, 196.
10. Sandra Gilbert and Susan Gubar, *The Madwoman in the Attic: The Woman Writer and the Nineteenth-Century Literary Imagination* (New Haven, Conn.: Yale University Press, 1979), 373.
11. See, for instance, Sarah Lewis, *Woman's Mission* (London: John W.

Parker, 1839).
12. Fraser, *Charlotte Bront*, 329.
13. See also pp. 315, 328–30.
14. Stevie Davies, *Emily Brontë* (Hemel Hempstead: Harvester/Wheatsheaf, 1988), 118.
15. See Janet Gezari (ed.), *Emily Jane Brontë: The Complete Poems* (Harmondsworth: Penguin, 1992), 182, 15.
16. Lyndall Gordan, *Charlotte Brontë: a Passionate Life* [1994] (London: Vintage, 1995), 189.
17. Elizabeth Gaskell, *North and South* [1854–5] (Oxford: Oxford World's Classics, 1998), 190. See Barbara Leah Harman, 'In Promiscuous Company: Female Public Appearance in Elizabeth Gaskell's *North and South*', *Victorian Studies* 21/3 (1988), 351–74 and *The Feminine Political Novel in Victorian England* (Charlottesville and London: University of Virginia Press, 1998), for an extended contrast between these scenes.
18. Edward Chitham (ed.), *The Poems of Anne Brontë: A New Text and Commentary* (Basingstoke: Macmillan, 1979), 163.
19. Glen, *Charlotte Brontë*, 188, quoting Kingsley's *Yeast.*

CHAPTER 5. *VILLETTE*

1. Kate Millett, *Sexual Politics* [1969] (New York: Avon, 1971), 192.
2. George Eliot, Letter to Mrs Bray, 15 February 1853, quoted in Miriam Allott (ed.) *The Brontës: The Critical Heritage* (London: Routledge & Kegan Paul, 1974), 192.
3. Sandra M. Gilbert and Susan Gubar, *The Madwoman in the Attic: The Woman Writer and the Nineteenth-Century Literary Imagination* (New Haven: Yale University Press, 1979), 399–400.
4. [Harriet Martineau], unsigned review in *The Daily News* (3 Feb. 1853), 2; quoted in Allott (ed.), *The Brontës*, 172.
5. Matthew Arnold, Letter to Mrs Forster (14 April, 1853); quoted in Allott (ed.), *The Brontës*, 201.
6. Gilbert and Gubar, *The Madwoman in the Attic*, 399.
7. Millett, *Sexual Politics*, 192, 200.
8. Heather Glen, *Charlotte Brontë: The Imagination in History* [2002] (Oxford: Oxford University Press, 2004), chs 7 and 8.
9. The term 'Hypochondriasis' figured in Patrick Brontë's much-annotated copy of Thomas John Graham's *Domestic Medicine* (1826). See Sally Shuttleworth, *Charlotte Brontë and Victorian Psychology* (Cambridge: Cambridge University Press, 1996), for an extensive discussion of Charlotte Brontë's familiarity with nineteenth-century psychological terminology.

103

10. Tim Dolin, 'Introduction', V. p. xi.
11. See Christine Alexander and Margaret Smith (eds), *The Oxford Companion to the Brontës* (Oxford: Oxford University Press, 2003), 521–3.
12. The paragraph includes half-quotations from Acts 27: 20.
13. See Shuttleworth, *Charlotte Bront and Victorian Psychology*, 226–7, for details of Elizabeth's story.
14. Ibid. 222.
15. Robert Heilman, 'Charlotte Brontë's "New" Gothic in *Jane Eyre* and *Villette*' [1958], in Miriam Allott (ed.), *Charlotte Brontë: 'Jane Eyre' and 'Villette'*, Casebook series, (Basingstoke: Macmillan, 1973), pp. 195–204, 204.
16. Shuttleworth, *Charlotte Bronte and Victorian Psychology*, 224.
17. Glen, *Charlotte Brontë*, 223.
18. Harriet Martineau, unsigned review, *Daily News* (3 Feb. 1853), 2; in Allott, *The Brontës*, 172–3.
19. Mary Jacobus, 'The Buried Letter: Feminism and Romanticism in *Villette*', in Mary Jacobus (ed.), *Women Writing and Writing About Women* (London: Croom Helm, 1979), 42–60, 48 (quoting Freud).
20. Ibid. 54.
21. Gilbert and Gubar, *The Madwoman in the Attic*, 432.
22. Shuttleworth, *Charlotte Bront and Victorian Psychology*, 243.

CHAPTER 6. READERS AND REPRODUCERS

1. Sheila Greenwald, *It All Began with Jane Eyre: or, The Secret Life of Franny Dillman* [1980] (Harmondsworth: Penguin, 1988). This charming book for teenagers follows a girl who begins by trying to shape her life to match Jane Eyre's, but ends by writing her own story, with the title words as her opening.
2. Peter Brooks, *The Melodramatic Imagination* (London and New York: Yale University Press, 1976).
3. The text of Courtney's play is included in Patsy Stoneman (ed.), *Jane Eyre on Stage, 1848–1898: An Illustrated Edition of Eight Plays with Contextual Notes* (Aldershot: Ashgate Press, 2007).
4. Ibid. 81.
5. Ibid. 82.
6. Ibid. 108.
7. See ibid.
8. Ibid. 329.
9. Ibid. 421.
10. Brooks, *The Melodramatic Imagination*, 26.
11. For more details about the derivatives mentioned in this chapter,

see Patsy Stoneman, *Brontë Transformations: The Cultural Dissemination of 'Jane Eyre' and 'Wuthering Heights'* (Hemel Hempstead: Harvester Wheatsheaf/Prentice Hall, 1996); 'The Brontë Myth' in Heather Glen (ed.), *The Cambridge Companion to the Brontës* (Cambridge: Cambridge University Press, 2002), relevant entries in Christine Alexander and Margaret Smith (eds), *The Oxford Companion to the Brontës* (Oxford: Oxford University Press, 2003) and 'Adaptations, Prequels, Sequels, Translations', in Marianne Thormählen (ed.), *The Brontës*, Authors in Context series (Cambridge: Cambridge University Press, 2012).

12. Margaret Oliphant, 'Modern Novelists – Great and Small', *Blackwood's Magazine* lxxvii (May 1855), 557–9; in Miriam Allott (ed.), *The Brontës: The Critical Heritage* (London: Routledge & Kegan Paul, 1974), 311–14, 311–12.

13. Ibid. 312.

14. Margaret Oliphant, on 'sensational novels', *Blackwood's Magazine* cii (September 1867), 257–80 in Allott, *The Bronts*, 390–1, 390.

15. Ibid. 391.

16. Winifred Hughes, *The Maniac in the Cellar: Sensation Novels of the 1860s* (Princeton: Princeton University Press, 1980), 9. For more details about '*Jane Eyre* and the woman's novel, 1850–70' see Stoneman, *Brontë Transformations*, 16–33.

17. *Emma* is reprinted in *Charlotte Brontë: Unfinished Novels*, ed. Tom Winnifrith (Stroud: Alan Sutton, 1993), 94–113.

18. Clare Boylan and Charlotte Brontë, *Emma Brown* (London: Little, Brown, 2003).

19. Elizabeth Gaskell, *The Life of Charlotte Brontë* [1857] ed. Angus Easson (Oxford: Oxford World's Classics, 2009).

20. Elizabeth Gaskell, letter to George Smith, 31 May [1855], in *The Letters of Mrs Gaskell*, ed. J. A. V. Chapple and Arthur Pollard [1966] (Manchester: Manchester University Press, 1997), 345.

21. Allott, *The Brontës*, 38.

22. May Sinclair, *The Three Brontës* (London: Hutchinson, 1912), 21.

23. May Sinclair, *The Three Sisters* (London: Hutchinson, 1914).

24. Patricia Ingham, *The Brontës*, Authors in Context series (Oxford: Oxford World's Classics, 2006), 224.

25. Virginia Woolf, *A Room of One's Own* [1928] (Harmondsworth: Penguin, 1970), 74.

26. Mills & Boon, established in 1908, was purchased by Harlequin Enterprises in 1971.

27. Germaine Greer, *The Female Eunuch* [1970] (London: Granada, 1980), 180.

28. Tania Modleski, *Loving with a Vengeance: Mass-Produced Fantasies for Women* [1982] (New York: Routledge, 1988).

29. Ibid. 69.
30. Elaine Showalter, *A Literature of their Own: British Women Novelists from Brontë to Lessing* [1977] (London: Virago, 1978), 118, 122.
31. See Stoneman, *Brontë Transformations*, 204, for more detail on this production.
32. Sandra M. Gilbert and Susan Gubar, *The Madwoman in the Attic: The Woman Writer and the Nineteenth-Century Literary Imagination* (New Haven, Conn.: Yale University Press, 1979), 339. This book is discussed at more length in Ch. 3.
33. Matthew Arnold, Letter to Mrs Forster (14 April 1853); quoted in Allott, *The Brontës*, 201; Polly Teale, *Jane Eyre* [1998] (London: Nick Hearn, 2001).
34. The libretto to Michael Berkeley's opera, by David Malouf, was published by Vintage (London, 2000).
35. Jean Rhys, *Wide Sargasso Sea* [1966] (Harmondsworth: Penguin, 1983).
36. Elaine Showalter, 'Literary Criticism', *Signs* 1 (1975), 435–60, 435.
37. Polly Teale, *After Mrs Rochester* (London: Nick Hern, 2003).
38. Paula Rego, *Jane Eyre* (illustrations) intro. Marina Warner (London: Enitharmon, 2003).
39. Paula Rego quoted in T. G. Rosenthal, *Paula Rego: The Complete Graphic Work* (London: Thames & Hudson, 2003), 166.
40. Ibid. 176.
41. D. M. Thomas, *Charlotte: the Final Journey of Jane Eyre* (London: Duck Editions, 2000).
42. Jasper Fforde, *The Eyre Affair* (London: Hodder & Stoughton, 2001).
43. Laura Joh Rowland, *The Secret Adventures of Charlotte Brontë* (New York: Overlook, 2008) and *Bedlam: The Further Secret Adventures of Charlotte Brontë* (New York: Overlook: 2010).
44. Robbie Kydd, *The Quiet Stranger* (Edinburgh: Mainstream, 1991).
45. Emma Tennant, *The French Dancer's Bastard* [2002] (London: Maia Press, 2006).
46. Claire Moise, *Adèle, Grace and Céline: The Other Women in Jane Eyre* (College Station, Tex.: Virtual Bookworm, 2009), jacket blurb.
47. Melanie M. Jeschke, *Jillian Dare* (Grand Rapids, Mich.: Revell, 2009); Sherri Browning Erwin, *Jane Slayre* (New York: Gallery, 2010).
48. Margot Livesey, *The Flight of Gemma Hardy* (New York: Harper Collins, 2012).
49. Kay Woodward, *Jane Airhead* (London: Andersen, 2009).
50. Jennifer Vandever, *The Brontë Project* (London: Simon & Schuster, 2005).
51. Maya Angelou, *I Know Why the Caged Bird Sings* [1969] (London: Virago, 1984), 136.
52. Jeanette Winterson, *Oranges are not the only Fruit* [1985] (London:

Pandora, 1985), 28, 74.

53. Tsitsi Dangarembga, *Nervous Conditions* (London: The Women's Press, 1988), 93.

54. Lisa Evans, *Villette* (London: Oberon, 2005).

55. Mary Jacobus, 'The Buried Letter: Feminism and Romanticism in *Villette*', in Mary Jacobus (ed.), *Women Writing and Writing About Women* (London: Croom Helm, 1979), 42–60; Sally Shuttleworth, *Charlotte Brontë and Victorian Psychology* (Cambridge: Cambridge University Press, 1996), ch. 10; Heather Glen, *Charlotte Brontë: The Imagination in History* [2002] (Oxford: Oxford University Press, 2004), chs 7 and 8.

Select Bibliography

WORKS BY CHARLOTTE BRONTË

Editions of the Novels

For each novel, the Oxford Clarendon edition provides the definitive text, and the Oxford World's Classics editions, which use the Clarendon text and notes, are the recommended paperback versions. The Penguin editions are also good and the Everyman and Norton editions have substantial editorial material including extracts from critical essays.

Early and Unfinished Writing

Alexander, Christine, *The Early Writings of Charlotte Brontë* (Oxford: Blackwell, 1983). A thorough account of all the early writing.
——— (ed.), *An Edition of the Early Writings of Charlotte Brontë* (Oxford: Shakespeare Head Press, 1987, 1991). This definitive text only covers the years 1826–35 so far.
——— (ed.), *The Brontës: Tales of Glass Town, Angria, and Gondal: Selected Writings* (Oxford: Oxford World's Classics, 2010). A selection of early writings including some by Branwell, Emily and Anne.
Glen, Heather (ed.), *Charlotte Brontë: Tales of Angria* (Harmondsworth: Penguin, 2006). Includes five of Charlotte's 'novelettes' written 1838–9.
Winnifrith, Tom (ed.), *The Poems of Charlotte Brontë* (Oxford: Shakespeare Head Press, 1984).
——— (ed.), *Charlotte Brontë: Unfinished Novels* (Stroud: Alan Sutton, 1993). Includes 'Willie Ellin', 'Ashworth', 'The Moores' and 'Emma'.

Letters and Essays

Lonoff, Sue (ed. and trans.), *Charlotte Brontë and Emily Brontë, The Belgian Essays: A Critical Edition* (New Haven and London: Yale University Press, 1996). Meticulous transcriptions of the essays, showing M.

Heger's corrections, with translations and commentary.

Smith, Margaret (ed.), *The Letters of Charlotte Brontë*. 3 vols (Oxford: Clarendon Press, 1995–2004). The most complete and authoritative text.

———— (ed.), *Selected Letters of Charlotte Brontë* (Oxford: Oxford University Press, 2007). A manageable selection from the complete edition.

BIOGRAPHY

Barker, Juliet, *The Brontës* [1994] (2nd ed., London: Abacus, 2010). The most comprehensive and authoritative biography of the whole Brontë family.

Fraser, Rebecca, *Charlotte Brontë* (London: Methuen, 1989). A readable modern life.

Gaskell, Elizabeth, *The Life of Charlotte Brontë* [1857] ed. Angus Easson (Oxford: Oxford World's Classics, 2009). Written by someone who knew Charlotte, this readable work is the main source for many subsequent biographies.

Gordon, Lyndall, *Charlotte Brontë: A Passionate Life* (London: Vintage, 1995). Imaginative exploration of Charlotte's inner life.

CRITICISM AND REFERENCE

Alexander, Christine and Margaret Smith (eds), *The Oxford Companion to the Brontës* (Oxford: Oxford University Press, 2003). An encyclopedic and authoritative work.

Allott, Miriam (ed.), *Jane Eyre and Villette: A Casebook* (Basingstoke: Macmillan, 1973). An anthology of criticism up to 1970.

———— (ed.), *The Brontës: The Critical Heritage* (London: Routledge & Kegan Paul, 1974). An essential anthology of nineteenth-century reviews and criticism.

Barnard, Robert and Louise Barnard, *A Brontë Encyclopedia* (Oxford: Wiley-Blackwell, 2007). Meticulous, readable entries.

Boumelha, Penny, *Charlotte Brontë*. Key Women Writers series (Hemel Hempstead: Harvester Wheatsheaf, 1990). A thoughtful feminist account.

Eagleton, Terry, *Myths of Power: A Marxist Study of the Brontës* [1975] (3rd ed., Basingstoke: Palgrave Macmillan, 2005). A landmark study.

Gilbert, Sandra M. and Susan Gubar, *The Madwoman in the Attic: The Woman Writer and the Nineteenth-Century Literary Imagination* (New Haven: Yale University Press, 1979). An innovative and challenging feminist reading.

Glen, Heather, *Charlotte Brontë: The Imagination in History* [2002] (Oxford: Oxford University Press, 2004). An exhaustive and engrossing account of Charlotte Brontë's work in the context of contemporary culture.

—— (ed.), *Jane Eyre*, New Casebooks series (Basingstoke: Macmillan, 1997). An excellent anthology of late-twentieth-century criticism.

—— (ed.), *The Cambridge Companion to the Brontës* (Cambridge: Cambridge University Press, 2002). A collection of general essays.

Hoeveler, Diane Long and Beth Lau (eds), *Approaches to Teaching Charlotte Brontë's Jane Eyre* (New York: MLA, 1993). Practical accounts of teaching in different situations.

Ingham, Patricia, *The Brontës*, Authors in Context series (Oxford: Oxford World's Classics, 2006). An excellent introduction to the social and cultural context.

Lodge, Sara, *Charlotte Brontë: Jane Eyre: A Reader's Guide to Essential Criticism* (Basingstoke: Palgrave Macmillan, 2009). A clear and comprehensive guide.

Meyer, Susan, *Imperialism at Home: Race and Victorian Women's Fiction* (Ithaca and London: Cornell University Press, 1996). A thorough account of Brontë's use of colonial themes, including the juvenilia.

Michie, Elsie B. (ed.), *Charlotte Brontë's 'Jane Eyre': A Casebook* (Oxford: Oxford University Press, 2006).

Nestor, Pauline (ed.), *Villette*, New Casebooks series (Basingstoke: Macmillan, 1992). An excellent anthology of late-twentieth-century criticism.

Peters, Margot, *Charlotte Brontë: Style in the Novel* (Madison: University of Wisconsin Press, 1973). A unique exploration of Brontë's prose style.

Rubik, Margarete and Elke Mettinger-Schartmann (eds), *A Breath of Fresh Eyre: Intertextual and Intermedial Reworkings of Jane Eyre* (Amsterdam: Rodopi, 2007). Covers later material than Stoneman.

Shuttleworth, Sally, *Charlotte Brontë and Victorian Psychology* (Cambridge: Cambridge University Press, 1996). A fascinating account.

Stoneman, Patsy, *Brontë Transformations: The Cultural Dissemination of 'Jane Eyre' and 'Wuthering Heights'* (Hemel Hempstead: Harvester Wheatsheaf/Prentice Hall, 1996). The most complete account of Brontë derivatives in all media.

Thormählen, Marianne (ed.), *The Brontës*, Authors in Context series (Cambridge: Cambridge University Press, 2012). Numerous short essays on general topics.

Index

Abel, Elizabeth 100, 101
'Acton Bell' xi, 22, 57, 64, 65, 100
Adams, Judith 96
Africa x, 4, 8, 14
Alexander, Christine xiii, 3, 10,
    98, 99, 101, 104, 105, 108, 109
Allott, Miriam 86, 100, 101, 102,
    103, 104, 105, 106, 109
Amyes, Julian 93
Angelou, Maya 96, 106
Angria x, xiii, 9, 10–11, 13, 17, 18,
    24–5, 30, 42, 48, 98, 99, 100,
    101, 108
Arnim, Elizabeth von 88
Arnold, Matthew 63, 86, 103, 106

Bailey, Hilary 94
Barker, Juliet xiii, 5, 49, 52, 65,
    98, 109
Bennet, Kimberley A. 94
Berkeley, Michael 91, 94, 106
Birch-Pfeiffer, Charlotte 81, 82
Blackwood's Edinburgh Magazine 3,
    7, 9, 11, 102, 105
Bluebeard 43, 89
Bonaparte, Napoleon 6, 7, 9
Boylan, Clare 85, 95, 105
Braddon, Mary Elizabeth 83
Branwell, Elizabeth ('Aunt
    Branwell') ix, x, 2, 19, 20
Brontë, Anne ix, x, xi, 1, 2, 3, 9,
    13, 17, 19, 21, 22, 23, 29, 59,
    60, 61, 64, 65, 66, 98, 99, 100,
    103, 108
    Agnes Grey xi, 19, 23–4, 29, 64,
    99, 100; The Tenant of Wildfell
    Hall xi, 100
Brontë, Charlotte
    Caroline Vernon 16–17, 31;
    Emma xi, 85, 105, 108;
    'Farewell to Angria' x, 17–18,
    24; 'Frances' 23; 'Gilbert' 23;
    Henry Hastings 12, 31; Jane
    Eyre x, xi, xiii, 1, 30–47, 48, 49,
    53, 54, 55, 61, 63, 64, 67, 77,
    79–96, 101, 102, 104, 105, 106,
    109, 110; Mina Laury 10, 99;
    The Professor xi, xii, xiii, 23-9,
    30–1, 33, 34, 36, 39, 53, 66, 100;
    Roe Head Journal 15; Shirley
    ix, xi, xiii, 7, 12, 24, 50–62, 64,
    65, 66, 78, 96; Stancliffe's Hotel
    12; Villette xi, xiii, 63–78, 84,
    85, 96, 97, 104, 107, 109, 110;
    'The Wife's Will' 23; 'The
    Wood' 23
Brontë, Elizabeth ix, x, 1
Brontë, Emily Jane ix, x, xi, 1, 2,
    3, 9, 13, 16, 17, 19, 20, 21, 22,
    23, 57, 58, 59, 60, 62, 64, 98,
    99, 100, 103, 108
    Wuthering Heights: xi, 23–4, 64,
    89, 100, 101, 105, 110
Brontë, Maria (daughter): ix, x, 1
Brontë, Maria (mother): ix
Brontë, Patrick: ix, x, xii, 2, 5–7,

9, 21, 25, 50, 78, 84, 85, 98, 99, 102, 103
Cottage Poems ix, 100; *The Maid of Killarney* ix, 100; *The Rural Minstrel* ix, 100
Brontë, Patrick Branwell (known as Branwell): ix, xi, 1, 3, 8, 9, 12, 13, 15, 17, 21, 27, 29, 59, 98, 100, 108
Brooks, Peter 79, 82, 104
Brougham, John 80
Broughton, Rhoda 83
Brussels x, 19–20, 23, 24, 66–7
Bulwer-Lytton, Edward 11
Byron, Lord George Gordon 9–11, 27, 42, 50, 58, 99
Childe Harold's Pilgrimage 10; *Don Juan* 10, 11; *Turkish Tales* (*The Bride of Abydos; The Corsair; The Giaour; Lara*) 10, 42

Catholics, Catholicism 4, 5, 6, 27, 69–71, 74
Catholic Emancipation Bill 4, 6
Chartist revolt 50, 52
Church of England 5, 6, 57, 70
Clarke, Zelah 93
Clergy Daughters' School, Cowan Bridge ix, 1–2, 35
Coleridge, Hartley 21
Courtney, John
Jane Eyre: or, the Secrets of Thornfield Manor 80, 102, 104
Cowan Bridge: *see* Clergy Daughters' School
Craik, Dinah Mulock 82, 83
'Currer Bell' xi, 22, 31, 57, 65, 100

Dalton, Timothy 93
Dangarembga, Tsitsi 96, 107
Davies, Stevie 57, 103
Dickens, Charles 25, 49, 51, 79
David Copperfield 25, 79; *Hard Times* 51
Disraeli, Benjamin 49

Dolin, Tim xiii, 104
Donizetti, Gaetano
Lucia di Lammermoor 91–2

Eagleton, Terry 19, 25, 33, 99, 100, 101, 109
Easson, Angus xiii, 105, 109
Eliot, George 63, 103
'Ellis Bell' xi, 22, 57, 58, 64, 65, 100
Erwin, Sherri Browning 95, 106
Evans, Lisa 96, 107

Fassbender, Michael 94
Fforde, Jasper 95, 106
Fontaine, Joan 88
Foucault, Michel 70
Fraser, Rebecca 52, 54, 102, 103, 109
Fraser's Magazine 61
Freud, Sigmund 39, 40, 44, 75, 86–7, 88, 91, 101, 104
Fukunaga, Cary 94

Gainsbourg, Charlotte 93
Gaskell, Elizabeth xi, xiii, 2–3, 5, 7, 13, 49, 50, 51, 57, 59, 65, 82, 83, 85–6, 98, 103, 105, 109
The Life of Charlotte Brontë xi, xiii, 2, 85, 105, 109; *Mary Barton* 49; *North and South* 59, 83, 103
Gezari, Janet xii, 98, 103
Gilbert, Sandra M. and Susan Gubar 39, 53, 63, 77, 91, 101, 102, 103, 104, 106, 109
Glass Town x, xiii, 8, 9, 10, 13, 98, 108
Glen, Heather 11, 16, 17, 25, 52, 53, 61, 64, 72, 96, 97, 98, 99, 100, 101, 102, 103, 104, 105, 107, 108, 110
Gondal x, xiii, 13, 17, 98, 108
Gordon, Lyndall 58, 109
Great Exhibition 65

Green, Dudley 99
Greenwald, Sheila 96, 104
Greer, Germaine 88, 105

Haworth ix, x, xi, 1, 5, 12, 20, 49,
   64, 84, 96
Heger, M. Constantin x, xi, 20,
   21, 58, 73, 109
Heger, Mme Zoë 20
Heilman, Robert 71, 104
Hinds, Ciaràn 94
Holtby, Winifred 89–90
Hughes, Winifred 84, 105
Hurt, William 93

Ingham, Patricia 87, 105, 110
Ireland, Irish xi, xii, 5–6, 98, 84

Jacobus, Mary 75, 77, 97, 104, 107
Jeschke, Melanie M. 95, 106
John Bull 3, 51

Kavanagh, Julia 82–3
Kay Shuttleworth, Sir James 65
Kingsley, Charles
   The Saint's Tragedy 69; *Yeast*
   61, 103
Kydd, Robbie 95, 106

Leeds Intelligencer 3, 51
Leeds Mercury 3, 51, 52
Lewes, George Henry 49, 52, 66
Lewis, Sarah 102
Livesey, Margot 95, 106
Lonoff, Sue 20, 99, 108
Luddite rebellion ix, 7, 50, 52,
   102

Malouf, David 91, 106
Mann, Delbert 92, 93
Martineau, Harriet 63, 66, 73,
   103, 104
Maurier, Daphne du 88–9
Mellor, Kay 94
Meyer, Susan 42, 102, 110

Millett, Kate 63–4, 103
Mills & Boon (Harlequin) 47, 88,
   105
Milton, John 57
Modleski, Tania 89, 105
Moïse, Claire 95, 106
Morton, Samantha 94
Mudie's circulating library 24

Nelson, Lord Horatio 6
New Zealand 12, 21, 60
Newby, Thomas xi, 24
Nicholls, Arthur Bell xi, xii, 84
Nightingale, Florence 34, 95, 101
Northangerland, Earl of
   (Alexander Percy) 9, 16–17,
   100
Nussey, Ellen x, xi, 12, 18, 65, 74,
   85
Nussey, Henry x

Oliphant, Margaret 47, 83–4, 102,
   105
Orders in Council 7, 50, 61

Palmerston, Lord 6
Pell, Nancy 39, 101
Peters, Margot 101, 110
Pilgrim's Progress 9
Pryce, David x

Ratchford, Fanny 11, 99
Rawfold's Mill ix, 7, 50
Regency 9, 11
Rego, Paula 93, 106
Revelation, Book of 9
Rhys, Jean 41, 92–3, 106
   Wide Sargasso Sea 41, 92–3, 106
Rigby, Elizabeth (Lady Eastlake)
   18–19, 48, 55, 99, 101, 102
Robinson family xi, 21
Roe Head School x, 12–15, 50
Rosengarten, Herbert xiii
Rowland, Laura Joh 95, 106

Scarborough xi
Schreiner, Olive 58
Scott, George C. 93
Scott, Sir Walter 9, 91
Sewell, Elizabeth 18, 99
Shakespeare, William 9, 53
    Coriolanus 53
Shewell, Debbie 92
Showalter, Elaine 91, 92, 106
Shuttleworth, Sally xiii, 70, 71,
    77, 97, 101, 103, 104, 107, 110
Sidgwick, Mrs x, 16
Sinclair, May 87, 105
Smiles, Samuel 25
Smith, George (Smith, Elder &
    Co.) xi, 24, 31, 48, 49, 65, 66,
    71, 72, 85
Smith, Margaret xiii, 99, 101, 104,
    105, 109
Southey, Robert 9, 21, 22, 39
Spivak, Gayatri Chakravorty 41,
    42, 102
St John's College, Cambridge ix,
    5
St Paul 57
Stephens, Toby 94
Stevenson, Robert 88
Stonegappe x, 16

Taylor, Elizabeth 89
Taylor, Martha x, 20, 52
Taylor, Mary x, 12, 20, 21, 56, 60
Teale, Polly 91, 93, 106
Tennant, Emma 95, 106
Thackeray, William Makepeace
    30, 49, 65, 66, 77
Thomas, D. M. 94, 106
Thormählen, Marianne 101, 105,
    110
Thorp Green xi, 21
Tighe, Thomas ix, 5, 6
Townshend, Charles 11–12, 16

Trollope, Fanny 49, 51

Unitarian Church 59
United Irishmen 6
Upperwood House x, 18

Vandever, Jennifer 96, 106
Victoria, Queen 9, 30, 95
Victoria Theatre 48, 80

Wasikowska, Mia 94
Waterloo 3
Weightman, William x, 20
Weldon, Fay 91
Welles, Orson 88, 93
Wellesley, Arthur (Marquis of
    Douro) 10; *see also* Wellington,
    Duke of
Wellesley, Charles 11, 12
Wellington, Duke of (Arthur
    Wellesley) 3–4, 6, 8–9, 10, 15,
    48, 50, 102
White, Mrs x, 18
White, Susanna 94
Williams, William Smith 48, 49,
    54, 57, 58, 65
Willing, James 81, 102
Wills, W. G. 81–2
Wilson, Ruth 94
Wilson, William Carus 35
Winnifrith, Tom 22, 24, 100, 105,
    108
Winterson, Jeanette 96, 106
Wiseman, Cardinal Nicholas 70
Wood, Ellen 83
Woodward, Kay 96, 106
Wooler, Margaret x, 12, 15, 48, 50
Woolf, Virginia 38, 87, 101, 105

York, Susannah 93
Yorkshire ix, 1, 3, 6, 7, 50, 102
Young, Robert 94